DETOUR
MONTANA

—DETOUR—
MONTANA

HISTORY BY THE ROADSIDE

JON AXLINE

THE
History
PRESS

Published by The History Press
Charleston, SC
www.historypress.com

First published 2024

Manufactured in the United States

ISBN 9781467157650

Library of Congress Control Number: 2024931850

For Ellen

CONTENTS

CONTENTS

CONTENTS

INTRODUCTION

Montana's highways take motorists on a journey through the state's colorful history. People in the past were, as they are today, dependent on roads to get them from point A to point B. Accordingly, there is much more to see through the windshield than spectacular scenery and extraordinary geologic features. Most, if not all, of our current highways and roads originated hundreds of years ago as game trails that developed into roads used by Montana's Natives. The Native trails eventually transformed into the modern roads we all know today. This book concentrates on historic highways and other sites that are easily accessible and experienced from Montana's highways. More than a few curious characters and interesting events are included in this volume. No one book can even begin to do justice to the wide range of historical sites near Montana's highways. Indeed, since the late 1970s, the Montana Department of Transportation's (MDT) cultural resource staff and their term contractors have been documenting a wide range of archaeological and historic properties. For nearly half a century, MDT and its term contractors have found and documented in the neighborhood of three thousand archaeological and historic sites—all within a couple hundred feet of the highways. Not all are significant or very interesting; some are downright boring. But they all tell a comprehensive history of Montana's past. This and the previous volume, 2021's *Montana Highway Tales: Curious Characters, Historic Sites, and Peculiar Attractions*, barely scratch the surface of what Montana has to offer those interested in the state's history. The roadside historical markers provide an introduction, but there is much more to the story than what can be presented on the sign boards. Maybe that's why I love my home state so much and have never wanted to live anywhere else.

Included in this volume are places associated with the Lewis and Clark Expedition, territorial roads, bridges, highways and places connected to Montana's lively and exciting transportation history. Some places, like *Stoney the Bull* at Clearwater Junction, are well known to motorists, but information about them is sparse. Many of these chapters were originally published in the MDT's newsletter, *Newsline*, and have been expanded or revised for this book. Also included are sidebars about a few of the state's fascinating geological features and little scraps of information about individual historic properties, such as the Morelli Bridge, Interstate 90's massive Springdale Cut and the now disappeared railroad camp of Taft, to name just a few.

These places run the full gamut of Montana history, beginning with the Lewis and Clark Expedition and ending in the 1970s. What this book doesn't include are archaeological sites. They, too, are significant to our understanding of the Montana's past and its Natives, but I'm not anywhere near qualified to tell those stories and explain the reasons why those sites are important. Importantly, I don't want to reveal their locations or to say too much about them in the interests of preserving those places. There are several excellent archaeological histories of Montana that are still in print. I leave that subject to the experts.

This is not an attempt to look at Montana's past academically. All the chapters and sidebars were meticulously researched. The endnotes provide clarification for some of the things mentioned in these stories, but you won't find any other citations. There are two different types of histories. Some are written by professional historians and meant for other professionals or serious students of the subjects at hand. For others, history should be entertaining yet provide a lesson. History doesn't happen in a vacuum. Events are directly shaped by the things that happened before or concurrent with them. People cause history. A short bibliography is included at the end of this book. It mostly cites newspapers. The advent of Newspapers.com has certainly made researching history a lot easier, but it can also lead you down different rabbit holes to areas of interest you never even imagined. That, to me, makes history fun and exciting. Hopefully, this book will spark some interest in Montana history and lead readers to do their own research into the places and events that took place near their homes—whether in state or out of state. With that, enjoy this short trip through the state's past.

As every author is fond of saying, no book is a lone effort; this one is no different. Writing a history is often a team effort, in which an author relies on the scholars, colleagues, students and amateur historians who came before them. Other historians provide inspiration and, hopefully, the determination to do a good job telling the story authors want to tell. Historians also rely on other historians for ideas and advice on how to approach a subject. Although this book does contain original research, I was reliant on many others to help tell the stories. As always, I'm indebted to my coworkers at the Montana Department of Transportation, my home away from home for over three decades. The Montana Historical Society's Research Center provided a place of refuge for this author while researching many of the stories contained in this volume. The staff, including the now-retired Zoe Ann Stoltz, Roberta Gebhart, Rich Aarstad, Jeff Malcolmsen, Tom Ferris and many others, were their usual helpful selves, and I sincerely thank them. The Montana State Historic Preservation Office also provided invaluable assistance for this project. John Boughton and Kate Hampton are my partners in crime and beer. Also important were the staff members of the Montana School of Mines and Geology in Butte and the many many Montanans who contributed their expertise on the state's history. Chuck Rankin, Joan Brownell and the late Paula Petrik uncomplainingly (as far as I know) let me bounce many of these subjects off them while formulating the table of contents. Finally, my beloved wife, Lisa, has the patience of a saint. It's not easy being married to a historian. We can't help but dredge up the past.

I dedicate this book to my late colleague and dear friend Ellen Baumler. She read most of the chapters in this book while they were in draft form. Her excellent comments and suggestions made this a better book—with few, if any, passive voice sentences. She was an ace storyteller, and as we all know, history is a whopping good story. Godspeed my friend. I miss you.

1

A LARGE ROCK SURROUNDED
BY A HANDSOME PLAIN

Tower Rock

The United States celebrated the Lewis and Clark bicentennial in the early 2000s. In Montana, the years leading up to the bicentennial kept the many Montana chapters of the Lewis and Clark Bicentennial Commission busy identifying sites associated with the expedition and developing and installing interpretive markers along its route. All things Lewis and Clark were the order of the day regarding the state's history, especially after the 1996 publication of Stephen Ambrose's bestselling book, *Undaunted Courage*. Landscape features that could be positively identified from the captains' journals received particular attention, especially if they were easily seen from the highways. One such geological feature stands sentinel next to Interstate 15 a few miles south of the community of Cascade.

In May 1804, Meriwether Lewis, William Clark, twenty-eight soldiers, an African American man, boatmen and one dog left St. Louis for parts largely unknown. President Thomas Jefferson had directed Lewis to explore the territory acquired by the United States as part of the Louisiana Purchase. The president also hoped the expedition would find the long-hoped-for Northwest Passage. It was a scientific expedition with significant political ramifications. Along the way, the expedition picked up an interpreter, Toussaint Charbonneau, and his teenage Shoshone wife, Sacajawea. The Corps of Discovery spent the winter of 1804–5 at the Mandan villages on the upper Missouri River and then headed upriver into the unknown with the Pacific Ocean the ultimate goal. The flora and fauna encountered and geological observations made by Lewis and Clark on the northern Great Plains were staggering and surely overwhelmed the explorers as they slowly made their way across what would one day be known as Montana. By June 1805, the Corps of Discovery had reached the fabled Great Falls of the Missouri, a major obstacle to their passage upriver.

It took the expedition a month to portage around the Great Falls. On July 15, 1805, they once again proceeded upriver, passing the mouth of the Smith River that same day. The expedition camped near the present-day community of Ulm that night. After enjoying an early morning meal of seared bison entrails, Lewis, accompanied by George Droulliard and the "invalleds" John Potts and Jean Baptiste LePage, left the company to explore ahead, where the Missouri River entered the Adel Range of the Rocky Mountains. The Adels are the remnants of a volcanic pile that was active from about 75 to 55 million years ago. The range is a rugged landscape of laccoliths, with radial dikes extending from them and other stark remnants of explosive volcanic eruptions that occurred millions of years ago. The Adels provide a spectacular canyon bordering the Missouri River between Cascade and Craig along I-15. For Lewis and Clark, the Adels, as they do for motorists today, afforded a dramatic gateway to the Rocky Mountains.[*]

As Lewis and his companions neared the range, he described them as being "formed almost entirely of hard black grannite [sic] with a few dwarf pine and cedar scattered on them." The captain also noted the presence of a Native trail on the west side of the river. Lewis was the first to describe Pine Island Rapids, another significant impediment to river travel south of the Great Falls.

More important to Lewis was a rocky outcrop that bordered the rapids on the west. Lewis described:

> [It is a] *large rock of 400 feet high which stands immediately in the gap which the missouri* [sic] *makes on its passage from the mountains; it is insulated from the neighboring mountains by a handsome little plain which surrounds it* [sic] *base on 3 sides and the and the Missouri washes its base on the other, leaving it on the Lard. as it descends.* [This] *rock I called the tower.* [It] *may be ascended with some difficulty nearly to its summit, and from it there is a most pleasing view of the country we are now about to leave.* [From] *it I saw this evening immence* [sic] *herds of buffaloe* [sic] *in the plains below.*

---

* In 1991, University of Montana geologists David Alt and Donald Hyndman theorized that the Adel Range ten miles south of present Cascade were the true gates of the Rocky Mountains described by Meriwether Lewis in his journals. The volcanic features of the Adels more closely match Lewis's description than that of the present gates of the mountains north of Helena.

Tower Rock provided a dramatic gateway to the Rocky Mountains for the Lewis and Clark Expedition in July 1805. *Rob Park/MDT.*

Lewis scaled the southern promontory of Tower Rock to make his observations. The rock, which resembles a castle tower, afforded him an excellent panorama view of the Great Plains to the north. He wrote in his journal on July 16, "[It] may be ascended with some difficulty nearly to its summit, and from it there is a most pleasing view of the country." The north promontory is about 363 feet above the surrounding plain, while the south crag is 60 feet taller. After descending the rock, the party enjoyed an elk dinner and then suffered from the hordes of "musquetoes," which rendered sleep for the small party almost impossible.

Tower Rock is well known by Montana's first citizens, especially the Blackfeet. In addition to the Native trail, Lewis also noted the presence of several recently abandoned brush lodges. The rock was on an important trail system between the plains north of the Great Falls and the Helena valley. The Blackfeet considered Tower Rock a sacred place and conducted ceremonies there.

The significance of Tower Rock lies primarily in its importance to the Blackfeet and its association with the Lewis and Clark Expedition, specifically as an important point of transition between the Great Plains and the Rocky Mountains. On either side of the landform, the corps encountered a very different landscape, and up to this point, they had a relative familiarity with the territory based on maps, descriptions and information gathered at the Mandan villages. They knew, if only vaguely, what to expect in the way of landmarks and terrain after the Great Falls. Once they moved past the Great Falls, an important psychological turning point took place, as they left the familiarity of the Great Plains and entered the terra incognita of the Rocky Mountains.

Eighty-two years after Lewis and Clark, the Montana Central Railroad constructed its main line through the Missouri River Canyon along the east side of Tower Rock. James J. Hill and a group of Helena businessmen, including Charles Broadwater, established the railroad with plans to extend the St. Paul, Minneapolis and Manitoba Railroad to Great Falls and, ultimately, through the Montana Central, gain access to the lucrative Butte mines. The Montana Central completed the line to Helena in November 1887 and extended it to Butte the following year. Although there is no mention of Tower Rock in the historical record regarding the construction of the line, it appears the railroad had to blast a path for the tracks next to the geological feature on its southeast side.

The Montana State Highway Commission acquired Tower Rock from a private landowner in the 1960s to build I-15 between Cascade and Craig. The commission's agents had no idea what it had purchased. Fortunately, Lewis and Clark historians later notified the MDT about the significance of that particular geologic feature in time to celebrate the expedition's bicentennial. MDT later transferred ownership of the site to the Montana Department of Fish, Wildlife and Parks, which developed it into a state park. Tower Rock stands guard at the mouth of the Missouri River Canyon. It is a geological relic of the Corps of Discovery's epic journey across the unknown over two hundred years ago, and yes, it does look like a castle tower.

2

ROUGHING IT MONTANA STYLE!

Beavertown

Montana was once sprinkled with settlements that no longer exist and are mostly forgotten to history. They're nothing more than dots on old maps. Yet people once lived, raised their families, celebrated holidays and died in those long-forgotten places. In southwestern Montana, many of those specks on old maps served as stage stations on the roads that once connected the mining camps, agricultural settlements and Fort Benton to the outside world. For a time in the early 1860s, gold produced in Montana Territory was critical to the Union's Civil War effort and to the national industrial boom that followed the war. One of those forgotten dots on a map, Beavertown, functioned first as a mining camp, then as a stage station and, finally, a ranch. The now-jumbled collection of buildings standing near I-15 just south of Jefferson City was once an important stop on the road between Virginia City and Helena.

Pennsylvania native Milo Cortwright came to Montana from California in 1863. The next year, he and three other men discovered promising gold-, silver- and copper-bearing lodes in the mountains west of Beavertown Creek on the north side of the Boulder Divide near Jefferson City. The mother lode, however, proved elusive to them, and by February 1965, the *Montana Post* reported the camp was anything but prosperous, "a small cluster of cabins which appears to have entirely stopped growing." By late 1864, Beavertown contained only thirty-five male residents—it was hardly a booming mining camp.

In January 1865, the territorial legislature authorized Cortwright and his partners to form the Beaver Town Company on 160 acres of land "now occupied by said…company." Although many commentators agreed that the Cortwright Lode held promise, mining in the adjacent hills was sporadic with disappointing results. The "town," moreover, never amounted to anything more than a few decrepit cabins. A *Montana Post* correspondent wrote in February 1865 that Beavertown "seemed to be deserted," with "plenty of vacant cabins…to be found."

A major gold strike on Last Chance Gulch in 1864 caused a stampede to the new diggings and the establishment of Helena. Strategically located about midway between Alder Gulch and Fort Benton, Helena changed the travel dynamics in the region and quickly became a territorial transportation hub. Ox trains destined for Grasshopper Creek and Alder Gulch from Fort Benton utilized the roundabout way over the Mullan Road, later rechristened the Benton Road, to the Deer Lodge valley and then moved south to the mining camps. With the founding of Helena, the freighters established a more direct route from Fort Benton, south through the Prickly Pear valley, Helena, Boulder and then to Virginia City.

In May 1864, President Abraham Lincoln signed the Organic Act, which created Montana Territory. In October that year, the territory's citizens elected twenty men to represent them in the first territorial legislature held at Bannack during the winter of 1864–65. In addition to establishing the legal foundation for the new territory, the legislators grappled with other significant issues, including the creation of a road system. The lawmakers realized the importance of a good road network in the new territory, but funding it proved to be difficult. No property tax base existed to fund roads, bridges and ferries. Instead, the legislators hit on the idea of licensing toll companies to create a road system for them. To that end, the legislators chartered toll companies to construct and maintain a rudimentary transportation system in Montana.

On January 24, 1865, the legislature approved the license for the Prickly Pear and Virginia City Wagon Road Company to build and maintain a toll road from just north of Montana City south to Virginia City. The legislature authorized the toll road for ten years on the condition the tollkeepers maintain the route in good condition. In return, the legislature allowed the company to charge three dollars per wagon drawn by two animals and a dollar for each additional pair of animals. Horsemen paid fifty cents to use the road, as did each handler of a pack animal, and handlers paid twenty-five cents per head of loose stock. A six-team stagecoach would pay five dollars to navigate the toll road. The legislature permitted the company to build toll gates near Montana City and in the canyon three miles southeast of Boulder. Four stage lines eventually used the road: A.J. Oliver and Company, Wells Fargo, the Gilmer and Salisbury Overland Stage Company and the Utah and Montana Stage Company.

Beavertown's significance lay in its strategic location on the new toll road. It is unclear who established the stage station. An undated article in the *Montana Post* stated that "the old proprietor of the Beavertown ranch after a long and earnest struggle has sold out to [Rufus King] Emerson and [Richard] Jeffries." The newspaper indicated Emerson operated the Beavertown station in 1868, and he is listed in the 1870 census for Jefferson County as a "landlord." The census shows Ralph's wife, Nettie, was a "landlady."

In 1864, A.J. Oliver and Company established a stage line between Virginia City and Helena. Oliver stagecoaches ran triweekly stagecoaches between the two mining camps. Each coach boasted a six-horse team to shorten the 125-mile, fourteen-hour trip between the camps. Oliver sold out to Wells Fargo in 1866. Three years later, Wells Fargo sold its route to Gilmer, Salisbury and Company, which operated the stage line until the early 1890s. Like most stagecoach companies, Oliver, Wells Fargo and Gilmer and Salisbury built both change, or swing, stations and home stations along their routes. Men and women under contract to the stage

Time-consuming and uncomfortable, stagecoaches were reliant on a network of stations for fresh horses and dubious meals. *MHS Photograph Archives, Helena, JORCSL.*

companies established change stations about every 8 to 10 miles on the road. There, hostlers changed the stagecoach's one-, two- or three-horse teams. At swing or home stations, located every 50 miles on the road, passengers could get out of the cramped and overcrowded coaches, buy a meal and, if needed, obtain lodgings for the night. The station keepers also changed horses at the stations.

The Beavertown stage station functioned as a home station on the Helena–Virginia City Road. The station keepers were under contract to the stagecoach companies. Like many home stations, the Beavertown station proprietors consisted of a husband and wife. Rufus King and Nettie Emerson owned the station from circa 1864 to 1873, when they sold it to Sam and Kate Getts. They, in turn, sold it to Alex and Nellie Lux (or Looks) in 1877. The Luxes sold out to Michael and Ann O'Connell, the last proprietors of the stage station, in 1879.

The Beavertown stage station was typical of the times. In 1872, author Mark Twain described a home station on the Overland Trail between Missouri and California during a cross-country trip in 1861 in his book *Roughing It*:

> *The buildings consisted of barns, stable rooms for twelve or fifteen horses, and a hut for an eating room for passengers. The latter had bunks in it for the station keeper and a hostler or two. You could rest your elbow on its eaves, and you had to bend in order to get in at the door. In place of a window there was a square hole about large enough for a man to crawl through, but this had no glass in it. There was no flooring, but the ground was packed hard. There was no stove, but the fireplace served all needful purposes. There were no shelves, no cupboards, no closets. In a corner stood an open sack of flour and nestling against its base were a couple of black and venerable tin coffeepots, a tin teapot, a little bag of salt, and a side of bacon.*[*]

Twain's description of the stage station on the Overland Trail closely matches that of the Beavertown station.

Meals and accommodations at the home stations garnered much attention in regional newspapers. The fare in some stations could be dreadful. Twain observed, "Our breakfast was before us, but our teeth were idle." In 1876, the Utah and Montana Stage Company line, a subsidiary of the Gilmer and Salisbury Overland Stage Company, took special pride in the quality of the

---

[*] Twain, *Roughing It*, 18.

Built by an unknown person in 1865, the Beavertown stage station provided a welcome stop on the Helena–Virginia City line. *Photograph by author.*

meals at its stations, including Beavertown: "The home stations, supplying meals to the public, are as a rule kept at their best, conspicuous among them being those at Beavertown, Whitehall, Estes, Pleasant Valley, Corbett's, Harkness' and Franklin."

The Beavertown station provided passengers with meals and lodgings in addition to changing horse teams for the coaches. The log horse barn still stands at the Beavertown station. In March 1877, Alex Lux and his wife, Nellie, took over the operation of the Beavertown station from former stagecoach driver Sam and Kate Getts, who had operated the station since 1873. Getts likely built the two-story hotel that stands on the site. According to the *Helena Independent*, the Luxes "understood how a hotel should be kept, and travelers are assured of receiving the most courteous attention." During the couple's tenure, the site functioned not only as a stage station but also as an important local community gathering center. The Luxes welcomed a daughter into their family while tending the station.

Michael O'Connell purchased the stage station from Lux in April 1879. Born in Ireland in 1828, O'Connell moved to Helena sometime in the early 1870s and worked as a carpenter. He moved to Beavertown shortly after buying the establishment. O'Connell maintained the hostelry's reputation for fine food and commodious lodgings. The *Helena Weekly Herald* reported that he would "keep a first-class station in every respect, and we venture the assertion that stage passengers will not get a better meal…than will be served at the Beavertown station." In 1880, Beavertown counted a population of fourteen, including six members of O'Connell's family. His wife, Ann, was the only woman in the small community. Others living at Beavertown included a prospector, freighter, stock tender, laborer, teamster, two herders and a mining engineer.

The winds of change began to blow for the Beavertown stage station in August 1886, when engineers for the Helena, Boulder Valley and Butte Railroad Company surveyed the route for a new railroad that passed near the stage station. The proposed railroad, a subsidiary of the Northern Pacific Railway, provided a connection to the railroad's main line east of Helena and terminated at Calvin, a station that served the silver mines at Elkhorn about twenty-four miles southeast of Beavertown. The company began construction of the railroad in October 1886 and completed the line to Calvin a year later. The Montana Central Railroad completed its line from Helena along Prickly Pear Creek over the Boulder Hill to Butte in November 1888. With the completion of both railroads, both within sight of Beavertown, there was little need for the stage station.

Increasing traffic on the road between Helena and Virginia City compelled Sam Getts to construct an imposing "hotel" at Beavertown around 1875. *Photograph by author.*

Like many stage stations, Beavertown eventually transitioned to become a ranch. In 1906, Frank Erickson moved on to the old Beavertown stage station site. Born in Sweden in July 1864, Frank immigrated to the United State in 1882. He was in Montana Territory by 1887 and worked a few years as a miner before taking a job as superintendent of the Grey Eagle Mine at Basin. In 1897, Frank worked in nearby Wickes. He married Hedvig Maria Hager Bengtsdotter in Helena the same year. Hedvig immigrated to the United States from Sweden in 1894. She lived in Iron Mountain, Michigan, before moving to Marysville, Montana, in 1896. By 1900, Frank was serving as a mine foreman there. During their time in Wickes, the couple welcomed their seven children.

By 1930, Frank and Helvig; their sons Albert, Robert, Ernest and Edwin; their daughter Berna; and their daughter-in-law Bertha all lived on the ranch. The ranch was self-sustaining. The family raised potatoes and a large variety of root vegetables on site and stored them in a root cellar. The Ericksons also raised poultry, including a couple of turkeys. The dilapidated old stage station served as a chicken coop. The only items the family needed to go to the nearby town of Jefferson City or sometimes Helena for were staple items, such as coffee, spices, flour, Karo syrup and sugar.

Frank died in September 1937 and was buried in nearby Jefferson City. After his passing, the 1940 census indicates three sons, Albert, Robert and Edwin, as well as Frank's widow, Hedvig, remained on the ranch. The end of the decade witnessed several changes to the ranch. In 1948, Hedvig passed away at the age of seventy-six. She had been ill for several months prior to her passing. A year later, in June 1949, Eddie married June Rose Gasser in Helena. Eddie and June continued to live on and run the ranch. June Erickson, Eddie's wife, preceded Eddie in death, passing at the age of seventy-two in February 2002. After June's passing, Eddie continued to live on the ranch along with a friend who assisted him with the daily chores. Eddie passed away in Helena in December 2005. Since Eddie's passing, Beavertown has sat vacant. Eddie and June Erickson's tombstone in the Jefferson City Cemetery reads, "Last Residents of Beaver Town." The hotel currently has a vacancy.

3

ONE OF THE FINEST MOUNTAIN BOULEVARDS

Priest Pass

Our frontier forebears were no different from people today—they were always trying to find a better way of getting from here to there. Priest Pass is a good example of that mindset. With two good mountain passes west of Helena, one ambitious man saw an opportunity to add one more route to the growing network of roads that spread across the territory in the late nineteenth century. Valentine Thomas Priest was opportunist in the best frontier tradition. Although mistakenly called the county's "first road builder," Priest was, nonetheless, an important figure in the development of Helena because of his faith in the potential of the community.* Ultimately, the Priest Pass Road failed as a main thoroughfare between Helena and points west, but it is now a favorite backroad for many twenty-first-century motorists.

Born in Parishville, New York, in 1831, Valentine Priest operated a flour mill in Taylorville, Illinois, after marrying Celestia Sanford in 1857. While in Illinois, he contracted tuberculosis and went west in the hope the dry air would improve his health. Priest arrived in Montana in 1864 via the Bridger Road, the less contentious alternative to the Bozeman Trail. He spent nearly a year prospecting for gold in the Virginia City area and then returned

---

* It can be argued that, technically, Constant Guyot was the county's first road builder. He built a road from the Little Blackfoot River, across the continental divide at MacDonald Pass, to Ten Mile Creek in 1868. Prior to Guyot, John Mullan built a military road over the continental divide west of the Helena valley in 1860. But Lewis and Clark County didn't yet exist.

Valentine Priest built the third transcontinental divide toll road west of Helena. His wife and daughters collected tolls from 1880 to 1896. *MHS Photograph Archives, Helena, 944-454.*

to Illinois in 1865. For four years, Priest operated a hotel with his brother in Decatur. In 1869, Priest, along with his wife and two daughters, Millie and Alice, took the newly completed transcontinental railroad to Corinne, Utah, where they disembarked and traveled north by wagon to Montana Territory over the Montana-Utah Road. The family first settled in Grizzly Gulch, where Valentine worked for several years as a placer miner before establishing a sawmill in Colorado Gulch, west of Helena.

By 1878, Alexander MacDonald had hired Priest to manage his toll road over the Continental Divide west of Helena. Although local legend states that MacDonald sold the road to Priest, there is no evidence this ever occurred. Like many toll road managers in Montana Territory, Priest didn't take an active hand in the management of the MacDonald Pass Road. He left the collection of tolls to his daughters while he scoured the surrounding hills in search of gold. In 1879, Priest relocated a pass that had once been used by prospectors traveling to the Kootenai Country in the early 1860s. Because of the relatively low elevation of the pass (5,984 feet, compared to 6,320 feet at MacDonald Pass) and the potential for an easier grade, Priest terminated his employment with MacDonald to build a toll road over the rediscovered pass.

Helena civil engineer Benjamin Marsh surveyed a wagon route over Priest Pass in 1879. Priest began work on the road in September that year. Contractors' estimates for road construction were too high, so Priest decided to build the road with labor he hired or by letting smaller contracts. He managed to complete a rudimentary road over the pass by December that year. The *Bozeman Avant Courier* claimed the road was "highly praised by freighters," but it would take another eight months for Priest to officially complete construction of the road. In December 1879 and January 1880, Lewis and Clark and Deer Lodge Counties authorized Priest to establish toll gates on the road and charge the public for its use. Priest built a substantial two-story log house at the southern base of the pass near Sweeney Creek. From there, Millie and Alice earned ten dollars a month collecting tolls from sometimes difficult travelers, including a particularly obnoxious character named Calamity Jane.

Although newspapers published glowing reports about the easy grade and beautiful scenery of Priest's new road, it was not popular with everyone. Indeed, Richard Riddle, division agent of the Gilmer, Salisbury and Company's stage line, chose to keep the stage on the MacDonald Pass route. He did "not think as well of the new road as he had anticipated he would." Other travelers must have felt the same way as Riddle. Valentine placed

Priest's residence functioned not only as home for his family but also as a tollgate and local community center. *MHS Photograph Archives, Helena, 950-389.*

advertisements on an almost daily basis in the *Helena Independent* and *Helena Weekly Herald* urging travelers to use his road rather than the MacDonald Pass route. There is some indication, however, that Priest Pass had become the main road over the Continental Divide near Helena by the time Montana became a state in 1889.

Valentine Priest died of Bright's disease in Helena in January 1890. His widow, Celestia, continued to operate the toll road until she moved to Marysville in 1896. She died in Helena two years later. The Priests' residence, once a social center in the Ten Mile Creek valley, soon fell into decay. For a while, it functioned as a fox farm. But by 1939, it had all but disappeared.

The arrival of the automobile in Montana in the early twentieth century briefly injected new life into the aging road. Automobile touring had become an exciting recreational pastime for many Montanans in the years before World War I. Although all the state's counties levied road taxes on their citizens to improve and maintain their roads, the roads were not especially kind to automobiles. The counties could not keep up with deteriorating roads that were in desperate need of repair, much less upgrade them for the new mode of transportation. One avenue for improvements were the trail associations.

Before 1926, many of Montana's highways had names rather than numbers, their routes blazed by colorful symbols. Privately funded trail associations promoted them as tourist routes to the nation's national parks and other attractions. Avid automobilists subscribed to the trail associations, with their dues sometimes spent on road improvements. Oftentimes, local commercial clubs and chambers of commerce sponsored "trail days," where citizens volunteered to make road improvements. Ten auto trails crisscrossed Montana in 1917. Many of the associations published trail guides with details about road conditions and advertisements for businesses along their routes.

The Priest Pass Road seemed particularly well suited for inclusion in the auto trail system. The pass was over three hundred feet lower than MacDonald Pass and featured easier grades and fewer curves than either the MacDonald or Mullan Pass routes. It also showcased more spectacular scenery than the other roads. Simply put, Priest Pass had more tourist appeal than MacDonald or Mullan Passes. What seemed particularly attractive about the road to motorists was that it was relatively well maintained by Lewis and Clark and Powell Counties.* In 1915, the road was part of the Great White Way, a network of county roads that connected Yellowstone and Glacier National Parks. The trail association marked the road with distinctive white and blue trail signs.

Beginning in 1914, Lewis and Clark and Powell Counties initiated projects to improve Priest Pass. Lewis and Clark County chose to use both county jail inmates and private labor to work on its side of the road. Local rancher Bert Coty supervised the project. Construction of the road east of the Continental Divide proved to be an ordeal for Coty and his crews. The county had to delay work on the project to settle a right-of-way issue with an adjacent landowner. That postponed construction work until March 1915. It took the crews another six months to complete the project. Powell County elected to use convict labor from the state penitentiary on the west side of the pass. The convict crews proved to be much more efficient than the east side workers.

---

* The west terminus of Priests Pass was originally located in Deer Lodge County. In 1901, the state legislature created Powell County, thus placing the west side of the road under its jurisdiction.

Teenager Hart Van Riper stands under the sign marking Priest Pass and the Great White Way around 1920. *MHS Photograph Archives, Helena, PAc 2003-05 1.*

In June 1915, both counties made plans to celebrate the impending completion of the road and its addition to the Great White Way. On August 21, 1915, over five hundred people from Powell and Lewis and Clark Counties attended the reopening of Priest Pass. Led by a delegation of politicians and Good Roads activists, a lengthy caravan of automobiles chugged their way up the road from Lewis and Clark and Powell Counties and rendezvoused at a meadow on the pass for a good "old-fashioned basket lunch." The revelers were treated to a series of speeches, including one by Lewis and Clark County commissioner William "Good Roads" Biggs and another by the president of the recently formed Montana Automobile Association. The festivities ended with a concert by the Capital City Band.

The *Helena Independent* described the road as one of the "finest scenic routes" in the West. It eulogized Valentine Priest for daring to do what even "the railroads had not attempted—cross the Montana Rockies!" It compared him with vigilante hangman X. Biedler for his "fearlessness in the extreme." The newspaper also praised the road for its relatively gradual climb through spectacular scenery that could easily be accomplished by an automobile in second gear with only a few places that required it be made in first gear. To accommodate motorists, the counties constructed a series of spring-fed water systems along the road that provided water for overheated radiators.

The 1915 celebration was the high point of Priest Pass. In 1921, the Federal Bureau of Public Roads and Montana State Highway Commission selected MacDonald Pass as part of the Federal Aid Highway System. The designation made MacDonald Pass eligible for federal funds for improvements. Although MacDonald Pass was higher in elevation, the grades could be made less severe without so many curves. According to one source, the Priest Pass was infamous for its treacherous nature and its propensity for burning out the brakes of automobiles.

Today, Priest Pass is located in the Helena National Forest. Unlike MacDonald Pass, Priest Pass's alignment has changed little since 1915. The road provides recreational access to the national forest with few realizing the history behind this thrilling route across the Continental Divide. It is one of the few roads in Montana where one can still experience the excitement of driving a thoroughfare that has not changed since its construction. Evidence of the backbreaking work that went into building the road is still visible. Like MacDonald Pass, it provided an important link between Helena and other Montana communities. The proximity of MacDonald Pass to Priest Pass provides a fascinating contrast between a modern highway and a remnant from Montana's more rugged past.

MONTANA ROADSIDES

THE MORELLI BRIDGE

During the 1890s, Helena underwent a makeover as it transformed from a rough mining camp into a modern political and economic center in southwestern Montana. The process began in the 1880s with the arrival of the Northern Pacific and Montana Central Railroads. The rough, false-fronted commercial buildings and log cabins fronting Last Chance Gulch and its side streets gave way to brick and stone business blocks and substantial wood-frame residences. The city's infrastructure also improved with modern sewer and water systems, brick-paved streets and a bridge. It was during this time that Helena became the Queen City of the Rockies.

In 1892, the Helena City Council authorized the extension of Howie Street from a point near the intersection of Adams Street, south to the intersection of Donaldson Street, a street that no longer exists. The project included the construction of a ninety-six-foot-long bridge across Reeder's Gulch at the head of Reeder's Alley. The city intended the project to provide a connecting route between the First and Third Wards and provide an alternate route to the First Ward School and the Helena City Hall at the intersection of West Main and State Streets. The city also meant it to ease the traffic jams that hindered traffic on Last Chance Gulch. The *Helena Independent* reported that "people who wish to drive up Last Chance Gulch will soon have an opportunity to do so without going through [Park] Street on the crowded part of Upper Main Street."

James E. Norris supervised work on the bridge and the street improvements. The stone for the bridge likely came from the nearby Adami Quarry on Mount Helena. Stonemason Carlo "Charles" Morelli built the bridge's

Built in 1892 and named for a local stonemason, the Morelli Bridge is Montana's oldest surviving timber bridge. *Photograph by author.*

abutments and bents. City crews placed the deck on the structure and installed "solid wood sides" to prevent accidents of people "falling off" the bridge. When the bridge was completed on October 22, 1892, First Ward Alderman Jacob Post "sent up a box of cigars to the workmen." City engineer John Wade provided a progress report to the city council on April 11, 1893, for the completion of the approaches to the new bridge.

Morelli purportedly built the bridge based on the design of a similar structure in Italy. An ethnic Italian, Carlo Morelli was born in southern Switzerland in February 1858. He received his training as a stonemason in Switzerland. Morelli immigrated to the United States in 1891 and first appears in the Helena newspaper the *Independent* in early October 1892. In 1891, he married Virginia Vassalli, also a Swiss immigrant. The couple lived in a stone house about one block northeast of the Morelli Bridge site. The footpath between his house and the bridge still exists. It is not known how many buildings Morelli built in Helena before he passed away in September 1910.

With the completion of the bridge, work began in earnest on the three-hundred-foot-long rock cut north of the bridge and the gravel surfacing of Howie Street. A tragedy, however, marred the otherwise successful project. Just before quitting time on November 2, 1892, one of the timbers that supported the rock crusher's storage bin failed, dumping seven tons of rock onto Thomas Joyce and killing him instantly. A former miner, Joyce began working for the city on the project in early October and had been employed on the rock crusher for only two days when the fatal accident occurred.

Work stopped on the project in December or January because of inclement weather. It had not resumed by the March 1893 city council meeting. At that time, each of the seven wards in Helena was represented by two aldermen, with the city mayor, Arthur Curtin, presiding over the meeting. At the meeting, Howie Street was the main topic of discussion among the aldermen. Two weeks earlier, on March 14, alderman Jacob Walker introduced a resolution in the meeting to discontinue work on Howie Street until the street commissioner, Stephen Orr, could provide the council with an estimate of how much it would cost to complete the project. The Morelli Bridge had been completed in October 1892 and stood as a bridge to nowhere. The rock cut north of the bridge had not been completed, nor had the road yet been graded. The council passed Walker's resolution.

Some aldermen, however, were unsure about the resolution passed earlier in March, and the city council discussion soon revolved around rescinding the resolution to allow work to continue on the project. First Ward alderman Marcus Lissner argued that the "bridge and cut at Howie Street would open up a large portion of valuable territory in [his] ward. There were lots of people who wanted work and he was willing to stand his share of the taxes." Alderman Anthony Harrity agreed with Lissner but wanted set a limit on the project's expense. Mayor Curtin echoed the alderman's sentiment. Alderman Thomas Fuller also wanted to set a limit but stated the bridge was useless as it stood. He claimed that the tax revenues from the section served by the road and bridge would more than pay for the project in three or four years. In the end, the six aldermen, including Lissner, Post and Fuller, voted to continue the work on the project. Four aldermen voted against it; three were absent from the meeting. City crews resumed work on the street in the spring of 1893. The grading of Howie Street between Adams and Chatham Streets, encompassing the new bridge, occurred during the summer of 1893. The city completed the project at the end of August and installed wood sidewalks later that year.

Howie Street and the Morelli Bridge are infamous to Helenans of a certain generation. Local teenagers knew the steep grade of Howie Street as "Thrill Hill." An automobile headed uphill from the south at a high speed on Howie Street would hit the crest of the hill and "catch air" as it went over the top, landing just short of the Morelli Bridge. In the 1990s, the city lowered the crest of the hill and placed a stop sign at the crest. It was the end of a rite of passage for many Helena teens.

4

THE NOT SO FORGOTTEN DEAD

Helena's Poor Farm Cemetery

In the fall of 2022, the MDT's Geotechnical Engineering Unit conducted a ground penetrating radar (GPR) survey of the suspected Lewis and Clark County Poor Farm Cemetery on North Benton Avenue in Helena. The historical record indicates that the county utilized the site as a cemetery for its poor and indigent residents from 1890 to 1916. There are no marked graves at the site, and the exact number of burials there is a mystery. It was the intent of the GPR survey to confirm the presence of unmarked graves, if not the number of burials, in the survey area. The survey revealed the potential presence of graves within the old cemetery but could not confirm if the graves were occupied or the extent of the burial ground. The survey revealed the final fate of some of Helena's less fortunate citizens at the end of the nineteenth and beginning of the twentieth centuries.

In 1871, the county commissioners purchased Daniel Carpenter's 160-acre dairy ranch about one and a half miles north of Helena and established a "poor farm" at the site five years later. The county administered the facility and annually contracted with physicians to care for the site's patients and with private individuals to manage the operation. The county constructed a hospital at the site in 1876 and expanded the facility when Herman Gleason took over management of it in 1880. Many Helena physicians, including the county coroner, contracted their services with the county at the hospital. From 1876 to 1885, the poor farm consisted of several buildings, including a barn, and a 12-acre vegetable garden with some acreage devoted to wheat. The garden produced potatoes, turnips, rutabagas, cabbages, carrots and peas. Improvements at the site included fences, ditches, outbuildings and a separate building for the "mildly" insane.

The county contracted management of the poor farm to private individuals on an annual basis. Responsibilities for the superintendent included the sheltering and feeding of each individual at the farm along with the maintenance of the buildings on the site. Twice a year, a "grand jury" inspected county-owned property, such as the jail and the poor farm, and provided the county commissioners with a report on the conditions at those institutions. For many years, the jury seldom had much good to say about the poor farm other than that the "inmates" appeared to be comfortable and well fed. Every year, the jury complained the main building was badly located in a swamp that impeded the quick recovery of the patients in the hospital. Poor ventilation aggravated the crowded conditions in the building. A committee of three local physicians (two of whom had been employed by the county in previous years) conducted a further investigation of the operation in March 1884. The dispute between the committee and the hospital's doctor, R.F. Clark, played out in Helena's two newspapers. The committee accused Clark of not providing adequate care to the patients, neglecting the "requisite medical and surgical skill demanded by the miscellaneous and serious class of diseases and accidents that call for treatment" and administering medicine based on economy without regard to the suffering of the patients.

The population at the hospital and county hospital steadily grew, especially after the arrival of the Northern Pacific Railway in 1883. The railroad sparked an economic and population boom in Helena that saw its transformation from a mining camp to a modern city. It was soon clear to the commissioners that the hospital and poor farm buildings were badly located and inadequate for accommodating a growing population of the poor, indigent and sick dependent on the county. Hospital and poor farm manager H. Gleason divided patients at the facility into three groups: the aged and infirm, those suffering from disease or because of accidents and "victims of intemperate habits." The last group made up two-thirds of the facility's inhabitants.

It was not until late 1885 that the county commissioners advertised for the construction of a new county hospital at the poor farm. Helena contractors Alfred Bourk and Charles Newbury obtained the contract to build a palatial two-story brick building on higher ground southeast of the old hospital building. The new structure included hospital rooms and dormitories for the poor farm's male and female residents. Bourk and Newbury completed

The county hospital and poor farm provided a place of sanctuary and care for Helena's and the county's less fortunate citizens. *MHS Photograph Archives, Helena, Jorud Collection.*

the building in June 1886. Once an "object of scorn by passersby," the poor farm included a new hospital and barn and outbuildings on eighty acres enclosed by a pole and wire fence. That summer, the commissioners purchased acreage adjoining the poor farm "for interment purposes, the present cemetery being too small for the increasing demands upon it."

From 1880 to 1890, both of the area's local newspapers sporadically reported deaths at the poor farm. The newspapers reported thirteen out of the forty-seven deaths that occurred at the poor farm between 1881 and 1889. All of the reported dead were men, ranging in age from six to seventy-six. Miner Henry Juenger was found starving and near death in his cabin at Canyon Creek and was transported to the poor farm, where he soon died. James Conlin died of pneumonia, and Tom Conlan died of scarlet fever, both in 1882. Other deaths that occurred at the poor farm included that of Lillie Filmore, a prostitute who succumbed to syphilis in January 1888.

One death at the poor farm garnered special attention in newspapers and the grand jury report. In mid-February 1884, a fifty-year-old German immigrant, Reiker Leridae, fell into an abandoned mining prospect pit while walking to his boardinghouse from a local restaurant at night. Despite the freezing temperatures, he managed to survive for ten days before his landlord and a friend heard his calls for help and rescued him from the pit. His rescuers took Leridae, who was suffering from hypothermia and severe frostbite, to the county hospital. He lingered there for three weeks before he died of gangrene. According to the *Helena Weekly Herald*, a fellow patient tended to Leridae, but by the time the hospital superintendent notified the county physician, it was too late to save him.

By 1887, the county poor farm had become a showcase, frequently visited by newspaper reporters and private citizens. In July 1887, a reporter from the *Helena Independent* accompanied Dr. Daniel Carmichael, the county physician, on a tour of the facility. By then, the farm consisted of 160 acres that were suitable for irrigation. The poor farm had planted 50 of those acres in wheat, oats, potatoes and other vegetables. Although the hospital could accommodate fifty people aside from the caretakers, its average occupancy during the summer comprised around twenty full-time residents. The reporter carefully noted that the number of "inmates" increased during the winter by thirty-five to forty. In the summer, "the old bums and broken-down saloon loafers, who found the place a convenient winter asylum, have crawled out since summer came." The death of six-year-old Lewis Coombes from typhoid in 1887, however, revealed a serious problem at the poor farm: the site's septic system drained into the well that supplied water to the farm's residents. A grand jury report two months after Coombe's death stated that the jury's members were paralyzed by the smell at the farm and had to pinch their noses closed during their inspection. It wasn't until 1891 that the county connected the poor farm to the city water supply.

In response to the grand jury's complaints about the small size of the poor farm cemetery, the county commissioners investigated options for a new burial ground in July 1890. Because the county had run out of room at the poor farm cemetery, it buried indigents in a corner of the Benton Avenue Cemetery. The commissioners ordered county surveyor Benjamin Marsh and poor farm superintendent William Stuewe to lay out a twenty-five-acre plot in the northwest corner of the farm grounds. The commissioners discussed "removing the county poor already buried in the cemetery to a place selected at the poor farm." The commissioners, however, had grander plans than just establishing a new potters' field. Their plan involved retaining a quarter of the acreage as a potters' field, another quarter for graves and the remaining half for use as a public cemetery. The commissioners planned to sell lots to individuals and families as a revenue source for the county. The public could buy individual grave sites for five dollars, while entire lots would cost twenty dollars. The proposed move would eliminate the poor farm's problem with water overtopping a portion of the original cemetery and create a more healthful environment at the poor farm by removing the cemetery from the vicinity of the county hospital.

The county's decision to relocate the poor farm cemetery caused some public controversy. Opponents of the county's plan argued that the county was not in the business of managing a public cemetery and said it would put it in direct conflict with a private corporation, the Helena Cemetery Association (HCA). In September 1890, the HCA formally offered the county five acres at the new Forestvale Cemetery for use as a potters' field and for those who died at the county hospital and poor farm. The association's offer was not philanthropical, as it proposed selling the acreage to the county for $300 per acre. The proposal caused another stormy debate among the county commissioners and the public. The county countered the association's offer by tendering $150 per acre. If the association accepted the offer, the county would make arrangements to move the cemetery to Forestvale. If not accepted, the county would bury the indigent and poor at a new poor farm cemetery. But there would be no sales of plots and lots to the public.

The public and county's discussion about the cemetery and the HCA's offer peaked shortly before Christmas 1890. At a contentious meeting held on

The remains of around 320 people may occupy this 1.8-acre tract in a Helena subdivision. All the graves are unmarked. *Photograph by author.*

December 18, the commissioners deemed it not in the county's best interests to abandon the cemetery "until fully assured that it has been organized and ample substitute for a physical dying community to meet the requirements of the people." The board agreed that the current cemetery was not adequate to meet the poor farm's requirements and that arrangements would soon be necessary for a new burial ground. The public protested the HCA's proposal by presenting a petition, signed by 350 county residents, objecting to the county entering into an agreement with the association. By the end of the meeting, the county commissioners had declined the cemetery association's proposal and made plans to relocate the poor farm cemetery to an alternate site. The board hired Miles McInnis to move the bodies from old cemetery to new site and authorized a $230 payment for him to do so.

McInnis began moving coffins to the new site by late December 1890. The *Helena Independent* reported that "the bodies interred at the county poor farm are being removed. This is proving quite a task, as the ground is in a flat which is under cover of snow and water." Further, the newspaper article stated that "in removing a body, it was necessary to build a dam around the grave to keep water from pouring in the grave; water had to be bailed out to reach the body." The process was not without complaints. In a letter written to the newspaper by poor farm superintendent William Stuewe, he objected to malicious gossip surrounding the move, which he attributed to "malice on the part of persons interested in another cemetery." Stuewe addressed the issue of several white children's caskets being left on the ground at the old cemetery by claiming there were only twelve graves plagued by water on the grounds, not the thirty reported in a *Helena Weekly Journal* story.

During the winter of 1890–91, the county reinterred 80 sets of human remains at the second poor farm cemetery. This included the remains of indigent residents of the poor farm who had died between 1880 and 1890. Some of these individuals had died in Helena from a variety of causes, including alcohol poisoning, drug overdose, exposure and suicide. From 1891 to 1900, the county purportedly buried 357 bodies in the second cemetery on North Benton Avenue. The burials included the remains of 30 women, 22 infants, 12 children and 19 "John Does." There was no segregation of Black and Chinese remains. The county originally marked the burials with wooden crosses carrying the names of the deceased. All those markers have since disappeared.

In July 1900, the county established an official potters' field on a ten-acre plot across McHugh Lane from Forestvale Cemetery to the east and north of the Odd Fellows Cemetery. The county paid Steuwe and Evan J. Harris forty dollars an acre for the property. The purchase occurred only ten years after the county designated the acreage for the second poor farm cemetery. Although it had established the new potters' field, the county continued to use the second cemetery until 1916. From 1901 to 1916, the county interred 24 individuals, including 6 infants, at the poor farm cemetery. The last buried there was James Symons, a cook who died of pneumonia on June 1, 1916. At least 377 individuals may be buried at the poor farm cemetery or around its fringes.

The county poor farm operated at its original location into the twentieth century. The hospital expanded in 1899, with other outbuildings being built during the 1920s. The October 1935 earthquakes severely damaged the 1885 building. The county replaced it with a concrete building at 3404 Cooney Drive in 1937. Increasingly, the hospital functioned as a county retirement home for the elderly rather than as a county hospital. The commissioners moved the county hospital to a new site adjacent to St. Peter's Hospital in 1984. It now functions as a retirement home and rehabilitation center. The old poor farm site went into private ownership in the late 1990s after years of sitting vacant.

The City of Helena now owns the second cemetery site in the Stone Meadows Subdivision off North Benton Avenue. In 2008, a workman from Helena Sand and Gravel disturbed human remains associated with the cemetery while trenching for a water main in the new subdivision. The remains consisted of part of a lower jaw and a femur. The backhoe also unearthed the side of a wooden coffin buried three feet below the topsoil. The city reburied the remains in the trench. Hundreds of Helena's neglected citizens currently occupy space in a subdivision's designated open space. Their names might be known, but their stories are forgotten. These people's experiences in Helena, no matter how unpleasant or unsavory, are important to Helena's history.

5

A SUBSTANTIAL IRON AND STEEL STRUCTURE

The Dearborn River High Bridge

Montana is fortunate to have a wide variety of historic bridges scattered across its landscape. While not as impressive as the Brooklyn or Golden Gate Bridges, Montana's spans are representative of the evolution of bridge engineering from the late nineteenth to the early twentieth centuries. Except for a very few, the structures are utilitarian and generally lack any extraordinary engineering features. They were workhorses designed to facilitate the movement of people and goods to the state's railroad stations, towns and main highways. This is not to say that Montana doesn't proudly exhibit a few unusual bridges, a few of which are unique and, in at least two cases, the only ones of their kind in the United States. The Pugsley Bridge, a unique cable stay structure, is one such bridge. But perhaps the most famous of these structures in Montana is the Dearborn River High Bridge southwest of Augusta in north-central Montana.[*]

The bridge spans the old Pend d'Oreille Crossing on the north fork of the Dearborn River. In 1859, railroad surveyor P.M. Engel camped with a band of Pend d'Oreille Natives near the crossing during a December blizzard. The crossing reaches along the river bottom on the south side of the Dearborn, crossing the river immediately below the future bridge

---

[*] The other singular bridge is the Pugsley Bridge south of Chester in Liberty County. It is a one-of-a-kind cable stay structure that was built in 1950. It is described in detail in chapter 26 of *Montana Highway Tales* (The History Press, 2021).

location and then proceeding along the north side of the river east of the bridge; the route of the trail and the ford is still plainly visible both on the ground and in aerial photographs of the site. Although the crossing was used by the Pend d'Oreille and Salish people to access buffalo country from west of the Continental Divide, it is located well within the Blackfeet Natives' traditional territory. The Blackfeet wintered and hunted buffalo in this area and collected plants here during the late spring and summer months. The river bottom in the canyon at the crossing provided shelter to the Blackfeet as well as materials important to the maintenance of Native bands.

The Lewis and Clark Expedition passed by the mouth of a "considerable river" on their journey up the Missouri River in July 1805. Lewis christened it the Dearborn River in honor of U.S. secretary of war Henry Dearborn. On the return trip back to St. Louis the following year, Lewis took a shorter, alternate route that largely followed a Native trail through the Rocky Mountains to the Great Plains. After crossing over Lewis and Clark Pass, he struck the Dearborn River in the general area of the Dearborn River High Bridge on July 8, 1806. Lewis did not, at first, recognize it as the same river the group had passed the previous July, so he renamed it the Torrant River.

Since the Upper Dearborn River valley was jealously protected by the Blackfeet, American development of it didn't begin until after the Marias River Massacre was carried out by the U.S. Army under the command of Major Eugene Baker in January 1870. In the wake of the tragedy, the federal government reduced the size of the Blackfeet Reservation to a line north of the Sun and Missouri Rivers in 1871. Prior to this, the non-Native presence in the region was small, limited to a few trappers and traders and traffic on the Benton Road. With the removal of the Blackfeet, however, huge tracts of what had once been prime bison grazing territory opened up to American ranchers.

Deer Lodge rancher Conrad Kohrs drove the first cattle herd into the Upper Dearborn River valley in 1869. Others followed him in the mid-1870s, including David Auchard, the Clemons boys, Warren Gillette and Stephen Mosher. Through preemption, desert and timber homestead entries, they amassed huge tracts of land over which to run their cattle. Although they were isolated from the mining camps, these ranchers found lucrative markets for their cattle and sheep in Helena, Fort Benton and Virginia City. They also raised large horse herds to sell to the freighting and stage companies that crowded the Benton Road to the south. The completion of the Montana Central Railroad along the Missouri River in 1887 caused a boom in the settlement of the Upper Dearborn River valley. While the region was previously the domain of ranchers, its population increased as would-be farmers claimed 160-acre homesteads under the 1862 Homestead Act.

To serve the growing population in the region, local ranchers established post offices that became the nuclei of small communities. The Clemons Post Office, for example, opened in 1898 about two miles northwest of the future bridge site. The preeminent community in the region was Augusta. Established by J.D. Hogan in 1883, Augusta served as a trade center for area ranches. Unlike Clemons, the community experienced steady growth through the nineteenth century as the population of the region grew. Clemons steadily declined, losing its post office in 1925.

As the population of the Upper Dearborn River valley grew in the 1890s, so, too, did the need for an improved transportation system to allow easier access between Augusta, Craig and Wolf Creek. The 1872 General Land Office map showed no roads or bridges in the vicinity of the Dearborn River High Bridge. The ranches sprinkled across the region before 1887 did not require an extensive road system, as the ranchers typically drove their cattle to either Great Falls (after 1884) or Helena. With the arrival of the Montana Central Railroad in 1887, cattlemen needed reliable access to its stations at Craig and Wolf Creek.

By the early 1890s, the need for good roads had increased to serve the growing number of people in the region. Evidence suggests that area residents utilized the old Native trail known as the Pend d'Oreille Trail to cross the river at the ancient ford. In 1896, the Lewis and Clark County commissioners officially established a road between Augusta and Bean Lake that it later extended to include the old river ford. After the county established the road, the commissioners made plans to construct a bridge at the crossing. In late October 1896, the county commissioners contracted with Hugh and Thomas Kirkendall to grade "3,700 linear feet of county road…on both sides of the North Fork of the Dearborn River approaching [the] bridge site near the Pend d'Oreille Crossing." The Kirkendalls completed the road before construction began on the bridge.

On December 11, 1896, the county commissioners instructed county clerk Charles W. Clark to advertise for the construction of a 250-foot-long "deck" bridge at the Pend d'Oreille Crossing of the North Fork of the Dearborn River about two miles southeast of the Clemons Post Office. Bids for the bridge were due at the Lewis and Clark County Courthouse

The unique Dearborn River High Bridge afforded a much-needed connection for the ranchers on the Rocky Mountain Front to the Wolf Creek railroad station. *MDT.*

on January 13, 1897. On the morning of January 14, the commissioners reviewed the plans and specifications for the bridge. That afternoon, the commissioners opened the eight bids received for its construction. Proposals ranged from a high of $10,435, offered by the Milwaukee Bridge and Iron Works Company, to a low of $9,989, proposed by the King Bridge Company of Cleveland, Ohio. Commission chairman Elizur Beach rejected all the bids submitted for the construction of the bridge because they were too expensive.

The commission met again the following day with representatives of the bridge construction companies to reconsider the bids received for the bridge. The commissioners and county surveyor John Wade tweaked the design by shortening the structure and narrowing the width of the steel tube–type piers. Based on the changes, the eight firms recalculated the bids and again submitted them to the county commissioners for consideration. This time, the commissioners liked the design submitted by the King Bridge Company the previous day for the bridge. But the commissioners felt King's amended bid of $9,150 was still too high. They did, however, negotiate a lower price with the King Company agent M.A. Adams. Consequently, the commissioners awarded the bridge contract to the King Bridge Company for its twice amended bid of $9,000 on January 16. The commissioners set a deadline of June 15, 1897, for the company to complete the structure.

Sometime between March 10 and March 15, 1897, the King Bridge Company shipped the steel and iron for the bridge to Wolf Creek, Montana, over the Montana Central Railroad. Unlike most of the bridge construction companies, the King Bridge Company also fabricated bridge components in its Cleveland, Ohio factory. The bridge's steel components arrived at Wolf Creek in May. Teamsters then hauled the bridge's components to the construction site about thirty miles northwest of the railroad station. Work on the bridge proceeded without incident.

The high bridge is the last of its type remaining in the United States, a pin-connected Pratt half-deck truss bridge. *MDT.*

The King Bridge Company had largely completed the bridge by the time it submitted its final bill for the structure on July 1, 1897, two weeks after the county's deadline. Consulting engineer George Reeder and county surveyor John Wade refused to accept the structure on the county's behalf because of two deficiencies in the bridge: the ends of the deck planks had not been sawed off to a uniform length and the steel pier caissons had not been completely filled with concrete, as stipulated in the plans and specifications for the bridge. Within a couple weeks, however, the problems had been remedied, and the county accepted the bridge from the bridge company.

The Dearborn River High Bridge has historically served the farmers and ranchers along the front range of the Rocky Mountains in northern Lewis and Clark County. The bridge provided access to the Great Northern Railroad spur at Augusta and the Montana Central line at Wolf Creek. From about 1897 to the early 1930s, it functioned as one of two vehicular routes between Helena and Great Falls. Today, most of the traffic over it is from area residents and recreationists utilizing the north fork of the Dearborn River. The Dearborn River High Bridge is located on the old road between Helena and Great Falls, now called Secondary 435.

The Dearborn River High Bridge is a pin-connected Pratt half-deck truss bridge. This means the deck is connected midway on the trusses instead of at the bottom or top chords, as it is typically done. Instead of rivets, the bridge is held together by steel pins. Fabricators in those days manufactured the steel bridge components at one of many factories in the east and Midwest. The companies assembled the structures on site to make sure everything fit specifications and then dissembled and shipped them to the construction site, where the contractors reassembled the structures. The pin connections facilitated the process.

The bridge is the last structure of this type remaining in the United States. In 2003, the Montana Department of Transportation rehabilitated the structure. It replaced the original rubblestone abutments and pier footings with concrete etched to simulate the original rubblestone abutments. Other improvements included straightening and tightening the truss members with new pins installed where necessary. The work also involved installing a new deck and crash-resistant aluminum guardrails to simulate those on the original structure. Lastly, the contractors repainted the bridge in its original Venetian red color. The bridge is listed in the National Register of Historic Places.

MONTANA ROADSIDES

THE WICKEDEST CITY IN AMERICA—TAFT

Few boomtowns in the American West could justifiably claim the title of the wickedest city in America, but the town of Taft on the Milwaukee Road Railroad may have earned that distinction. Construction camps followed the railroad as it pushed its way west to the foot of the Bitterroot Mountains in the first decade of the twentieth century. The St. Paul Pass Tunnel through the Bitterroot Mountains was the last link in the Milwaukee's Pacific Coast Extension. The railroad established construction camps on the east and west sides of the mountains to build the tunnel.

The tunnel was the reason for Taft's existence. The railroad completed approach work on the east and west sides of the pass in 1906, and boring of the tunnel began on both sides of the Bitterroot Range the following year. Progress was slow, with laborers averaging around six feet of excavation each day. Workmen from across the United States, Canada and Europe labored day and night for a paltry $2 a day. The subcontractors on the project, including Street and Lusk, deducted room and board from the workers' wages. The workers who handled the explosives, called "coyote men," received the highest pay: $3.25 a day. The men spent their wages in Taft's ubiquitous saloons, gambling dens and brothels. In February 1909, the tunnel crews "holed through" the mountain; three months later, they completed the 8,771-foot-long tunnel. The Milwaukee Road began regular service on its Pacific extension later that year.

Named for then–secretary of war William Howard Taft, the camp seemingly grew overnight, as laborers, businessmen and prostitutes flocked to the tunnel

Railroad construction camps were notorious dens of violence and debauchery. While short-lived, Taft was worse than most. *MHS Photograph Archives, Helena, Harry English Collection.*

construction site in early 1907. The camp consisted of two railroad tracks with a row of saloons, gambling houses, a ramshackle hotel, a theater, a drugstore and a general store on one side running parallel to them. The company hospital stood on a hill behind the main street adjacent to the cemetery. The cabins, tents, dugouts and wikiups that housed the workers were scattered around the town. It will never be known exactly how many people lived in Taft. Estimates range as high as two thousand during the boomtown's peak, but that's just a guess. Like the populations of mining camps before it, Taft's population was transient and its job turnover high. One thing is sure: drinking, gambling and lawlessness reigned supreme in Taft, and it soon gained a reputation as a "plague spot of vice."

The closest law enforcement to Taft was one hundred miles away in Missoula. One resident, Edith Shussler, later wrote in her reminiscence, *Doctors, Dynamite and Dogs*, that "murders, fights and shootings spelled the normal, for the day when nothing of the sort occurred was indeed rare." Local folklore suggests there were five prostitutes in Taft for every working man. After one spring thaw, residents found more than a dozen bodies in the nearby ravines or behind the saloons. Attempts to clean up Taft were met with resistance and, in fact, caused the debauchery to worsen. A fire in November 1908 failed to dampen camp activity; it slowed down only long enough for the burned buildings to be replaced. Taft was not a family town.

With the completion of the St. Paul Pass Tunnel in 1909, Taft's inhabitants drifted away in search of new opportunities. A catastrophic forest fire in 1910 leveled what remained of the camp. Prohibition and the establishment of U.S. Highway 10 in the 1920s sparked a rebirth of the town. By 1962, it comprised a few cabins, a bar and a hotel. Interstate 90 paved over the townsite. Taft stood at the approximate site of the Taft Interchange on I-90. Today, all that remains of the wickedest city in America is the recently rediscovered cemetery. It may hold the remains of at least 320 individuals and, quite possibly, more.

6

BLAZING A GOOD ROAD

Yellowstone Trail Signs in Deer Lodge

P hysical traces of the Yellowstone Trail are still present in Montana. Formed in 1912 by a group of South Dakota businessmen, the auto trail, one of the first in the United States, provided a connection between Minneapolis–St. Paul, Minnesota, and Yellowstone National Park. In 1915, the trail expanded to the West Coast at Seattle and eventually connected to Plymouth Rock on the East Coast. The 3,719-mile-long road was the first American interstate highway. The term *highway* gives the route too much credit. The Yellowstone Trail was a series of interconnected dirt- and gravel-surfaced county roads. Maintenance was left up to the counties, and at annual trail days, local supporters of the road would repair and improve it. The Yellowstone Trail Association was active in all the states through which the trail passed. It vigorously petitioned state highway commissions for improvements and published trail guides to direct motorists along its length and report on trail conditions. The association blazed the trail with bright yellow chrome circles with black lettering and arrows that kept motorists on the right road. Those blazes, while common at one time, have now become exceptionally rare, especially in Montana.

On the west bank of the Clark Fork, just south of the old Montana State Penitentiary and next to the former Milwaukee Road railyards, stands a red brick warehouse. The historic Conley Street Bridge spanned the river a few yards to the east. Built by convict labor in 1912, the reinforced concrete bridge once provided access to supplies destined for the prison from the railyard. Sometime after 1879, Deer Lodge grocer Peter Valiton purchased

Yellowstone Trail markers provided directions to travelers to keep them on the road. *Photograph by author.*

the land encompassing the future site of the warehouse. In January 1894, he sold the property to Frank Conley and Tom McTague. Five years prior to the purchase, in 1889, the newly christened State of Montana contracted with Conley and McTague to operate the former federal penitentiary in Deer Lodge.

Prison labor likely built the warehouse with bricks manufactured near the prison sometime between 1896 and 1900. In 1908, the state took over direct administration of the prison but kept Conley and McTague on to manage the facility; Conley acted as the warden of the institution. Prior to the state's action, the men formed the Conley and McTague Company in September 1907. In April 1911, the men transferred ownership of all their joint-owned property to the Conley and McTague Company. Even though Montana governor Joseph Dixon successfully managed to remove Conley from his positions of prison warden and chairman of the Montana State Highway Commission in 1921, Conley and McTague retained ownership of the warehouse.

The Yellowstone Trail crossed the Clark Fork from the east side via the Conley Street Bridge and then turned south for Anaconda and Butte in front of the warehouse. Painted on the southeast and northeast corners of the warehouse's façade and wrapping around to the north and south on the brick pilasters are Yellowstone Trail blazes. An "R" on the northeast corner directed traffic to the right over the bridge, while the southeast marker's "L" directed it to the left and south. Both are painted in the center of a black circle set in a chrome yellow background.

In 1915, the Yellowstone Trail Association hired William Warwick to travel the road and paint trail markers along its length. An article in the *Missoulian* reported on the official trail traveler's responsibilities. The association tasked him with painting not only Ls and Rs but also Xs for railroad crossings, Ds for "danger" and Ss for "slow." Warwick drove the trail in a Metz Roadster, a two-seat, four-cylinder automobile. The Yellowstone Trail blazes remain on the old warehouse building, a rare vestige from a time when motoring was new and road trips an adventure.

MONTANA ROADSIDES

PLACES THAT COULD NEVER BE FILLED

In October 1901, six-and-a-half-year-old Roy Hiber decided to take his pony for a ride, perhaps to visit his father, who was working on the family farm. Utilizing a homemade saddle with rope stirrups, the little boy and his pony trotted off across the family farm near Laurel. Something spooked the horse, and it bucked off the boy, whose foot got caught in a stirrup. The horse bolted across the field, dragging the boy behind it. By the time the animal stopped, it had dragged the child for well over a mile, "his brains having been dashed out and in addition he was practically disemboweled." His parents later found their little boy's body and buried him the next day.

That the boy was greatly loved by his family is evidenced by the headstone that marks his grave. The marble plinth reads, "A Place is Vacant in Our Home Which Never Can Be Filled." Atop it is a manufactured marble headstone with a carved bas-relief lily, which represents innocence and purity. The east face of the headstone is carved with "Roy Edward Hiber Died Oct. 7, 1901 Aged 6 Yrs. 6 mos. 26 Das." The grave is located in a field between old gravel pits several miles east of Laurel.

Roy was a member of the extended Hiber family. In addition to his mother and father, the family included brothers and sisters, aunts, uncles and cousins, all of whom lived in the area. The family began arriving in the area from the Midwest about 1896. Roy's mother and father set down roots near Laurel in 1898 or 1899. They had five children, including Roy, when they established themselves on property a few miles east of Laurel. Roy's grave was located on land owned by a fellow with the unusual name of Lake Huron Harriman. Lake Huron and

Roy Hiber, an uncle and two cousins are buried in a small cemetery east of Laurel. *Photograph courtesy of Scott Wagers.*

his brother, Lake Michigan Harriman, came to Yellowstone County a decade before the Hibers. Harriman obtained the land through a 160-acre homestead claim in February 1898. Because of his declining health, Harriman moved to Billings around 1900.

Hiber was buried next to an uncle who had died the year before. Will Consolver came to Laurel in 1899. He worked for and boarded with William Bode and his family in Laurel. In late 1900, doctors diagnosed him with a "brain abscess," an early term for a brain tumor, and gave him no hope for recovery. He died just before Christmas 1900. His family buried him at what was then known as the Allendale Cemetery. Allendale was, essentially, a paper community that never really existed. No houses, stores or post office were ever built there, just a flour mill that operated for only a couple years before it permanently closed.

The cemetery also holds the remains of the infant son of John and Pearl Cusick, who died in January 1907. He was Roy Hiber's cousin and Consolver's nephew. A little over a year later, in March 1908, William and Clara Jones laid to rest their ten-year-old daughter, Edith Rose, alongside her cousins and uncle. Born in Montana in 1897, Edith Rose died of diphtheria, an often fatal childhood disease at the time. Only Roy Hiber's grave is marked by a headstone, and it is enclosed by a wood picket fence.

Roy Hiber's extended family established the cemetery in anticipation of the construction of a new church adjacent to it. At the turn of the twentieth century, residents in the area approached Lake Huron Harriman about building a Presbyterian church on his property. Harriman agreed to the proposal and was prepared to deed land to the congregation. For reasons unknown, the congregation decided to build their new church at a different site about a mile to the east. The Canyon Creek Presbyterian Church opened its doors in 1909. The cemetery remained unassociated with a church or any other organization and was nearly forgotten until the late twentieth century.

In November 1958, the Montana Highway Commission bought the property containing the cemetery in conjunction with its interstate highway program. A year later, the commission awarded the Long Construction Company a project to construct a section of Interstate 90 between Mossmain and Billings. The contractor intended to utilize the property as a staging area, gravel source and office site. But before the project began, the contractor's foreman, Foster Oliver, had a task to perform: make sure that the cemetery wouldn't be disturbed by the construction activity in the area. He had the cemetery fenced off with barbed wire. Oliver also imposed a one-hundred-yard buffer around the burial ground. The fence, while badly deteriorated, still encloses the cemetery.

The "discovery" of the cemetery raised questions about who and how many people are buried there. Roy Hiber's grave is marked, but the others are not. In 1959, *Billings Gazette* correspondent Charles Rightmire reported that he could discern two graves flanking Hiber's plot at the time of his visit. He believed there were two others buried there as well. A descendant of Hiber's, Orville Jones, recalled that there were five burials there and possibly a sixth. A little over two weeks after Rightmire's article appeared in the *Billings Gazette*, Roy Hiber and Will Consolver's niece wrote to the newspaper that four people were buried in the cemetery: Roy Hiber, Will Consolver, Edith Rose Jones and Frank Cusick.

The question remains: How many people are buried in this lonely little cemetery? In November 2023, the MDT conducted a ground penetrating radar (GPR) survey of the cemetery. Ground penetrating radar is an electromagnetic investigation method that works by sending out a radio signal at a certain frequency and dielectric constant. When this signal encounters soil or an object with a different dielectric constant, this signal is reflected back and appears on the GPR scan. In the case of this survey, materials of significance with a differing dielectric constant than the background will look white or black on an otherwise brown background. This makes it easy to identify materials that contain water, air or metal, as the dielectric constant of these materials is very different from that of typical soil. In the case of identifying unmarked graves that are over a century old, the materials remaining from these sites are essentially bones, decayed wood and remnants of clothing fibers. GPR has recently been used to identify potential graves at Helena's old poor farm cemetery (discussed in chapter 4) and at Boot Hill Cemetery in Billings Heights.

The electronic survey of the cemetery positively revealed the presence of three unmarked graves in addition to Hiber's marked grave. Two graves flank Hiber's plot. One is outlined in small stones and probably marks Consolver's interment. The others are Edith Rose Jones and Frank Cusick's graves. Curiously, the GPR survey strongly hints at the presence of a fifth grave. If so, that person's identity is lost to history.

7

A LOST COMMUNITY SHOWPLACE

Circle's Gladstone Hotel

A fascinating thing about eastern Montana's early twentieth-century history is the enthusiasm and optimism many people felt about their adoptive state and its newly established communities. Like the mining camps before them, communities didn't need much to get started, just an overwhelming belief in their future. Unlike the mining camps, however, communities had a sense of permanency in their growth, especially the many homestead towns of eastern Montana. The people who moved to these communities intended to stay and make new lives for themselves and their families, not move on at the smallest sign of waning resources or other opportunities. The homestead boom sparked a surge in community building from 1910 to 1918. The 1909 Enlarged Homestead Act promised 320 acres to anyone willing to stay on the land and make a go of farming on it. Fee title ownership and being in charge of their destiny were tremendous lures for people from the Midwest and industrial Northeast.

Community building usually began with someone who had a dream or, more likely, a railroad that wanted to build its customer base. Whether the advertisements for fertile land, plentiful rain and the potential for big profits were true or not, thousands of people responded to the call. Between 1910 and 1920, Montana's population jumped from 376,053 to 548,889. By 1915, eastern Montana was speckled with new communities that provided services to the homesteaders and access to the railroads. It was a family frontier with new communities catering to the needs of families. It was in Montana's rural east that the temperance movement grew and flourished. Some of the first businesses entrepreneurs built in many of these towns were hotels.

Circle in McCone County once lay within the range of the Mabray Cattle Company, which established its headquarters, the Circle Ranch, about two miles from the existing town. Its brand simply consisted of a circle, which later gave the community its name. Pete Rorvik arrived in the area in 1906 and opened a general store and post office to trade with the local farmers and ranchers. In 1914, the Great Northern Railway's Dakota and Great Northern Townsite Company platted a town that would be located on railroad's proposed Montana Eastern Railroad. The line, however, never reached Circle. The people who settled around Rorvik's operation moved two miles to the new townsite to be on the railroad that never came. The town grew substantially during the homestead boom but suffered when the boom collapsed in 1918. By 1920, Circle consisted, according to the local newspaper, of "three churches, two banks, two rooming houses, two newspapers, two doctors, two garages, the steam-heated [Gladstone] Hotel, several stores and five lawyers."

The post–World War I economic depression and drought ravaged McCone County and Circle. The county, like many eastern Montana counties, hemorrhaged its population. By 1930, after the Great Depression had begun, the county counted a population of 4,790 and Circle a population of 519. The community enjoyed a respite from the trials of the postwar depression in 1928, when the Northern Pacific Railway completed a branch line from Glendive to Circle and Brockway. Circle incorporated in 1929 and managed to build a water and sewer system during the ensuing Great Depression. In 1939, the Federal Writers' Project wrote that Circle was "one of the towns that retain some of the flavor of the old cattle country; the cowpunchers on its streets are not ornaments hired to impress romantic visitors." The discovery of oil southeast of the community in 1950 initiated another boom in the region.

In November 1915, the Dakota and Great Northern Townsite Company sold three town lots in the business district to Redwater Valley State Bank president Mark Thoreson and bank cashier Max Lehman. Two weeks later, the men transferred the property to the Gladstone Hotel Company. The company had incorporated two months previously, with Thoreson, Chester E. Ward and Joseph O'Keefe owners of the company. Ward operated the Glendive Bottling Works, and O'Keefe happened to own a liquor license. The hotel company planned to use O'Keefe's liquor license to operate a "high class bar" in the planned new establishment.

The Glendive *Yellowstone Monitor* announced in its September 30, 1915 issue that "a modern hotel building and bar for the Town of Circle is now a

With spacious guest rooms, a high-class bar and a restaurant, the Gladstone Hotel was an oasis on the Great Plains of eastern Montana. *Montana Department of Transportation.*

certainty, contractor Wallace Perham of this city having been awarded the contract last Saturday." The planned hotel would stand two stories in height with a full concrete basement "and constructed throughout with lumber." The builders contracted for the hauling of twenty-five loads of building material out of Glendive. Although Perham's contract specified that the project be completed by January 1, 1916, he told the newspaper that its completion would occur ahead of schedule. The hotel's business partners anticipated the cost of the new hotel at $9,000. When completed, the hotel sported twelve rooms, a bar and a restaurant.

Perham had completed much of the work on the building by mid-November. The "large crew of men" installed the exterior clapboard siding and painted the hotel. The interior work was well underway, and the plate-glass display windows were in place. The *Circle Banner* claimed, "We daresay it will be the finest hotel in the Redwater valley." The hotel's owners hoped to open the bar the following week and the hotel by Thanksgiving. Unfortunately, the furniture and other equipment failed to materialize. The hotel didn't open for business until Christmas Eve; the first guests checked in the following day. The hotel restaurant served an extensive Christmas meal that included roast beef, turkey, consommé, several styles of potatoes and a varied selection of delicious desserts.

The hotel company sold the operation to Chester Ward on July 25, 1916. The following day, Joseph O'Keefe contracted with Ward to buy the hotel, restaurant and bar. O'Keefe was to repay Ward $9,000 in monthly payments ending in July 1917. O'Keefe duly satisfied his obligation to Ward and obtained title to the property. A new state law, however, seriously impacted O'Keefe's operation. A referendum passed by Montana voters in November 1916 went into effect in December 1918, banning the sale of alcoholic beverages, a prelude to national Prohibition. The referendum shuttered the Gladstone's "high-class bar," with the result that an insurance agency moved into the bar's former space. New occupants of the building also included a physician who maintained an office in the hotel, a fortunate situation as the Spanish influenza pandemic hit Circle hard, as it did many other rural Montana communities. The Gladstone moved beyond its original mission of serving as a hotel when it functioned as a hospital for influenza victims during the winter of 1918–19. Room 7 served as the morgue. O'Keefe lost the property in 1919, perhaps because of the pandemic and his inability to legally sell alcohol. Chester Ward reacquired the hotel at a sheriff's sale held in July 1919. About a year later, in June 1920, Ward sold the property to Raymond Hildebrand, a Glendive lawyer. By January 1921, bank president Ambrose and Helen Eynon owned the hotel. They immediately transferred ownership to Jack Kendig on January 1, 1921.

Kendig, formerly a McCone County farmer, ran a real estate office from the hotel in addition to maintaining his hotel management responsibilities. In 1926, the Northern Pacific Railway investigated the possibility of building a branch line from Glendive through Circle to Brockway. The prospect of the railroad coming to Circle created a boom atmosphere and hype in the community. The *Billings Gazette* reported, "One of the first evidences of the anticipated growth of the city is the announcement that J.J. Kendig, proprietor of the Gladstone Hotel, will construct a 20-room addition to his establishment next spring." The Northern Pacific completed its branch line to Circle and Brockway in 1928. Kendig never added twenty rooms to his hotel.

Kendig and his wife, Gertrude, sold the hotel and café to former Lost Creek rancher George Fountain and his wife, Mamie, in July 1931. At the time of the sale, the Kendigs left Circle for Bellingham, Washington. It is likely the Fountains managed the hotel on Kendig's behalf. The 1930 census shows the couple and their daughter, Mary, living in the hotel. The Fountains ran the hotel and café, renaming it the Fountain Café. George retired in 1946. In January 1951, George and Mamie sold the property to Mabel Sullivan, the co-owner of the local abstract and title company. She immediately sold half interest in the property to Mark and Mary LaRowe;

Mary was the Fountains' only child (she'd married Mark LaRowe in 1938). The Fountains constructed the six-unit concrete block motel addition in 1948. In 1959, Mary LaRowe advertised the hotel and motel as being for sale. The advertisement stated that the hotel contained twenty-six modern rooms and a five-room apartment. A three-room house with a bath, full basement and two-car garage also stood on the property. The property failed to sell in 1959 or 1960. Mary LaRowe owned the property until the 1990s.

Over the years, the building housed an Italian restaurant and a home-style café in addition to the hotel. The café closed in the early 1980s and the hotel in 1995. Unfortunately, fire destroyed this significant Circle landmark in September 2023.

8

AN OLD COUNTY LANDMARK

Browne's Bridge

Bridges were an important part of Montana's territorial landscape beginning in 1864, especially during high-water events when fording a river or stream was dangerous or impossible. During the first territorial legislature from December 1864 to February 1865, the delegates chartered twenty-three toll companies, seven of which were made specifically for bridges. Succeeding territorial legislatures chartered more toll bridge companies. Over time, the bridges became local landmarks, centers of small communities and important for providing directions for travelers. A few of those old bridges, like Parson's Bridge, still give their names to localities in Montana and are the sites of modern bridges. Browne's Bridge crosses the Big Hole River about six miles south of the community of Melrose.

The first Browne's Bridge stood just upstream of the current steel bridge for over half a century in southwestern Montana. The current Browne's Bridge spans the river about forty yards downstream of the first bridge's site. In 1866, Fred Burr and James Minesinger obtained a license from the territorial legislature to build a toll bridge at this site. Joseph Browne, a miner and former vigilante, bought the bridge from the partners in 1870 and charged tolls for its use under a county charter until after the turn of the twentieth century. Browne's family collected tolls from travelers, while Joe tended his cattle ranch west of the bridge. The toll bridge was a popular stopping place on the road between Bannack and Deer Lodge. For a time, it had a post office, and Wells Fargo and Company kept a station at the bridge. After the completion of the Utah-Northern Railroad in 1881, the

Constructed of materials near at hand, the original Browne's Bridge was typical of toll bridges built throughout southwestern Montana in the 1860s. *MDT.*

bridge provided access to Browne's railroad station for ore mined in the Pioneer Mountains west of there. Beaverhead and Madison Counties jointly purchased the structure in 1911.

Joseph Browne was a Montana legend when he died in 1906. Born in the states in 1831, he headed west with other prospectors during the Pikes Peak gold rush in 1859. After two years of hard work there, Browne journeyed north to the Deer Lodge valley. When news of the gold strike on Grasshopper Creek reached him in July 1862, he was one of the first to reach the new mining camp of Bannack. Browne was a member of the vigilance committee that hanged the infamous sheriff and road agent Henry Plummer in January 1864. In addition to running his toll bridge and ranch, Browne served in the territorial legislature for Beaverhead County and was the adjutant general of the Montana National Guard. Browne and his wife, Agnes, developed Browne's Lakes as a mountain resort in the late 1800s. They built log cabins and boat landings and stocked the lakes with trout. The resort was a popular destination for Butte's gentry, including copper king William A. Clark.

By the early twentieth century, the old toll bridge had become rather run-down and decrepit. Browne hadn't done any significant maintenance work to it since the 1880s. By 1915, it had clearly seen better days. The *Dillon Examiner* wrote, "For the past few years the old Browne bridge, having fallen into disrepute on account of its age and perilous swaying, has been condemned as unsafe for public traffic." A fire had seriously damaged the center span of the log bridge, forcing the counties to close it. This didn't prevent people from driving their automobiles across it, however.

The 1915 Montana legislature passed a bill that mandated the Montana State Highway Commission create a bridge department to develop standardized bridge plans for use by the counties. The legislation also gave the bridge department oversight responsibilities for county-funded bridge projects on state-designated highways and required a highway commission "resident engineer" be present on bridge projects. In May 1915, the commission hired Charles A. Kyle as its first bridge engineer. Kyle came to the highway commission from Utah, where he designed bridges for the American Bridge Company. Over the next two months, Kyle developed standardized plans for steel truss, steel stringer, reinforced concrete and timber bridges. The highway commission required the counties use the standardized designs, but the counties were still responsible for financing the structures. State bridge engineers inspected the structures before the counties authorized payment to the contractors. During its first year, the bridge department oversaw the construction of seventy-one bridges in twenty-four counties, including one on the border of Beaverhead and Madison Counties—the new Browne's Bridge.

In September 1915, Beaverhead and Madison Counties awarded a project to Missoula bridge builder Obert E. Peppard to construct a modern steel structure to replace the old toll bridge. Kyle designed the riveted Warren through truss bridge in July 1915. Unlike the old log bridge, which accommodated wagons and horses, Kyle's new bridge was designed for automobiles. The *Dillon Examiner* claimed the new bridge would "be of

The current Browne's Bridge represented the most modern features in early twentieth-century bridge design. It is listed in the National Register of Historic Places. *Photograph by author.*

sufficient strength to bear the weight of a 20-ton steam roller and will be one of the heaviest bridges in the county, containing about 140,000 pounds of steel." Peppard diligently worked on the bridge through the winter of 1916 and completed it in late March. A few weeks later, high water destroyed the old toll bridge, which had become "a melancholy reminder of the passing of the old west and its pioneering men and their works."

From 1916 to 1928, the new steel bridge was located on the main road between Butte and Dillon. The bridge continued to function as a local community center. During Prohibition, moonshining occurred in the vicinity of the bridge. Mac's 3 Aces saloon hosted dances near the bridge in the 1930s. The current Browne's Bridge is a souvenir of an earlier time, when automobiles were new to Montana's roads. Browne's Bridge is the oldest highway commission–designed bridge still standing in the state and is listed in the National Register of Historic Places.

9

MOTORING IN STYLE

Montana's First Paved Highway

A frequent question received at the Montana Department of Transportation is: When was such-and-such highway paved? Usually, it's an easy question to answer, as most of the state's main highways were paved in the 1930s. The secondary roads came a little later, after World War II. Some secondary roads have never been paved and still have gravel surfaces. What was Montana's first paved highway? Now, that's a good question.

Although the highway commission conducted a few experiments with paved roads in the late 1910s, serious discussions about paving roads with cement did not begin in commission meetings until 1920. On one level, the highway commissioners were not particularly supportive of paving roads. The commissioners viewed paved roads as an extravagance the state could ill afford. Gravel- and scoria-surfaced roads, they believed, more than adequately served the needs of the state. Gravel was the preferred year-round surfacing. It was durable, drained water and was easy to repair. The highway commission's third biennial report stated, "Of all the 67,000 miles of public highway in the state probably not more than 100 miles carry a traffic which justifies immediate improvement with the so-called paved surface." The commission could rationalize concrete paving only on high-traffic roads or where local officials specifically requested its use.

But despite what the highway commission told the legislature in its 1920 biennial report, it made plans for an ambitious paving program. In February

1920, commission chairman Frank Conley authorized chief engineer John Edy to purchase cement from the Three Forks Portland Cement Company "for use in connection with proposed Federal Aid paving projects." The cement company, based at Trident, agreed to sell cement directly to the state at a reduction of thirty cents per barrel. By October 1920, the highway commission had awarded seventy-one projects to contractors in thirty-two counties for a total of 560 miles of road improvements. Of those roads, 502 miles would receive either an earth or gravel surface. The highway commission planned to pave the remaining 58 miles with either blacktop or concrete. Of the first ten paving projects, half involved paving city streets with cement.

The most ambitious projects involved the concrete paving of twenty-three miles of the Yellowstone Trail between Butte and Anaconda in Silver Bow and Deer Lodge Counties. On March 12, 1920, the highway commission awarded a project to Butte contractors Marco Medin, Dan Reardon and P.J. O'Brien to build nine miles of concrete-paved highway in Silver Bow County. The project began at the foot of Emmett Avenue and proceeded westerly to the county line. The contractors won the project with their low bid of $208,518, a hefty sum for a 1920s highway project. Medin began work on his section of the road on May 3. Five days later, the seventy-five men employed on the project went on strike. They declared an open shop and continued working on the project. The contractor began pouring concrete in July and had completed four and a half miles of paved road by October. Winter weather shut down the project for the season in mid-October.

In early April 1920, the highway commissioners let a contract to Clifton, Applegate and Toole of Missoula to concrete pave the twenty-six miles of the Butte-Anaconda Road in Deer Lodge County. The project began at the Anaconda city limits and proceeded "east as long as the money permitted." The contractor avoided the labor problems experienced by Medin. By October, Clifton, Applegate and Toole completed eight miles of the highway. In celebration of the completion of that section, 252 cars passed over the route after a fifty-four-gun salute (one for each Montana county at the time) and a few words spoken by Governor Sam Stewart.

The completion of the first mile of concrete road in Montana was newsworthy. The *Anaconda Standard* stated that Deer Lodge County was the first in Montana to open a section of paved highway and then predicted the road "to be the liveliest 26 miles of roadway in the Pacific Northwest!" Meanwhile, highway commission engineers made plans to eliminate a

This page: When completed in September 1921, the twenty-six-mile-long Butte-Anaconda Highway was the first Montana highway to be paved in concrete. *Photograph by author.*

dangerous at-grade crossing of the Milwaukee Road Railroad on the Deer Lodge/Silver Bow County line. Deemed too expensive for a concrete or timber overpass, the engineers, instead, realigned 5 miles of the highway to the south to avoid the railroad crossing. Unfortunately, however, the section was not immediately paved. This paving would not occur for another seven years.

The road contractors completed the first concrete-paved highway in Montana in September 1921. Christened the "Medin Highway" by the Silver Bow County commissioners in honor of Marco Medin, the highway was twenty-six miles in length and cost $40,000 per mile to build. The county and state split the cost of the project. A highway commission resident engineer named U.S. Marshall supervised the project for the state. When completed, the concrete road was eighteen feet wide, the concrete eight inches thick at the crown and tapering to six inches at the edges. The highway was flanked by three-foot-wide dirt shoulders. All culverts on the segment were made of reinforced concrete, and the Anaconda Copper Mining Company provided the gravel aggregate, which was crushed and "thoroughly washed" at the smelter. The *Anaconda Standard* wrote, "It is believed the success of the Butte-Anaconda concrete highway, the first in Montana, will result in considerable activity looking toward the construction of such roads throughout Montana during the years by counties assisted by the federal government."

Unfortunately, this was not immediately the case. Between 1920 and 1928, the highway commission awarded 254 projects to contractors to improve 913.5 miles of roads. Of those projects, only 15 consisted of concrete paving for a total of 38.48 miles. Most were urban paving projects. In 1928, however, the highway commission started an ambitious program to pave Montana's highways with road oil. A full road mix project involved mixing an asphaltic oil with crushed rock or gravel and blading it onto the gravel surface of the roadway, creating a hard blacktop surface. The federal "make work" programs of the Great Depression accelerated the road oiling program in Montana. Thus, by World War II, most of the state's primary highway system was paved. Improvements in bituminous paving materials after the war transformed the highway landscape in Montana.

The old Butte-Anaconda segment of U.S. Highway 10 still exists south of the I-15/I-90 corridor. You can still access it at several points. Until maybe fifteen years prior to this writing, the original concrete surfacing was still exposed. But it had become so badly cracked with large potholes that it more resembled the surface of the moon than a highway. Driving along it was difficult and hard on a vehicle's tires and suspension. Silver Bow and Deer Lodge Counties have since resurfaced the road with asphalt, preserving the first concrete-paved Montana highway beneath it.

10

DOC SIEGFRIEDT'S FOLLY

The Black and White Trail

In the early years of the twentieth century, Montana was full of men and women who promoted their communities' benefits to anyone who would listen to them. Perhaps the most enthusiastic and forthright of them was John Charles Frederick Siegfriedt. A physician by training, he was Carbon County's greatest and most enthusiastic booster in the first half of the twentieth century. He was a force of nature, and Doc Siegfriedt's influence still resonates in the county.

Born in Iowa in 1879, Siegfriedt earned his medical degree from the University of Illinois in 1902 and practiced medicine in North Dakota and at Wibaux, Montana, before moving to Red Lodge in 1904. Two years later, in 1906, he moved a few miles east to Bearcreek, a new coal mining camp, where he worked as a doctor for the Montana Coal and Iron Company. From a boardinghouse he converted into a private hospital, Siegfriedt treated coal miners and their families for three decades. Company manager William A. Romek later remembered him as being over six feet in height, blue-eyed and "somewhat bald." He "was friendly, gregarious, active in community affairs, fluent in conversation as he was very well informed on so many subjects."

Doc Siegfriedt was a Good Roads enthusiast at a time when good roads in Montana were rare. In May 1916, Siegfriedt organized and served as president of the Black and White Trail Association with headquarters in Bearcreek. It was one of many trail associations active in Montana in the 1910s and 1920s. Formed by local businessmen, commercial clubs and boosters, the associations designated and promoted routes between the

Bearcreek and Red Lodge physician Dr. J.C.F. Siegfriedt was a man of many interests, primarily Carbon County's economic opportunities. *Carbon County Historical Society, Red Lodge.*

national parks in an effort to draw tourists to their communities. Trail men advertised their businesses in pamphlets and brochures in the hopes that tourists would stop and spend money in their communities.

Unlike other organizations, though, the Black and White Trail Association did not include a national park or historic site on its route. Instead, it promoted a road from Columbus, through Red Lodge and Bearcreek, to Cody, Wyoming. At that time, there was no northeast entrance to Yellowstone National Park, a shortcoming that Siegfriedt and the trail association hoped to remedy. There was not much, in fact, to draw tourists to the trail. The Black and White Trail Association ballyhooed Rosebud Lake, fishing in the Absarokee and Red Lodge areas, the Elk Basin oil field in Wyoming and the coal mines near Bearcreek as attractions. If the trail was going to be successful as a tourist destination, it clearly needed better places to visit. The association adopted an optimistic slogan at its first meeting: "10,000 Strangers Over the Trail This Summer!"

In 1917, Siegfriedt proposed extending the trail over the Beartooth Plateau to Cooke City. The "Father of the Black and White Trail" campaigned hard on many levels for the extension. He appeared statewide before area chambers of commerce, commercial clubs, civic organizations and whoever would listen to him tout the benefits of the road over the plateau. His rhetoric consisted mostly of making Billings, Montana, and Cody, Wyoming, important gateways to Yellowstone National Park, with Cooke City functioning as a new entrance to Wonderland. Siegfriedt claimed the route would open an area of "unsurpassed beauty" to motorists and allow them to take advantage of the Beartooth's recreational resources, such as camping, hiking and fishing. He appealed to the National Park Service, saying the new road would remove truck traffic from Yellowstone and allow mining and logging in the Beartooth National Forest. During his many speaking engagements, Siegfriedt raised a substantial amount of money through public subscriptions to pay for the new road.

Importantly, Doc Siegfriedt petitioned the Montana State Highway Commission for its assistance in surveying and designing the new route. The enactment of the Federal Aid Road Act in 1916 provided money to the states for road construction. Montana's share of the federal money was $1.5 million. Under the terms of the congressional legislation, the federal government, through the U.S. Department of Agriculture, provided money to the states on a 50/50 basis. In Montana, the counties were responsible for providing the state's match for federal funds. The counties raised the match through bond elections, road taxes and public subscriptions. The road had to be on the state highway system to receive federal funds. Fortunately for Siegfriedt and Carbon County, the Black and White Trail had been on the system since 1914.

In 1917, the legislature reorganized the highway commission in the wake of the passage of the Federal Aid Road Act. The legislature increased the size of the commission from three to twelve (one man from each construction district), with three men sitting on the executive committee. The chairman of the executive committee, Montana State Penitentiary warden Frank Conley, was the only salaried member of the commission. A byproduct of the state reorganization was the creation of the Montana Highway Department. It was responsible for the survey and design of roads on the state highway system. The commission administered the department through a chief engineer. It also awarded contracts for road projects in the counties.

It is unclear how involved Siegfriedt was in the survey and design process for the extension of the Black and White Trail over the plateau. His involvement, however, came to a temporary end in October 1918, when he joined the U.S. Army's Medical Corps during World War I. By then, the "Fighting Mayor of Bearcreek" had earned a reputation of ridding the city of "disloyalists" and as a spreader of "real American propaganda." It is uncertain how he did this. Approximately one-third of Bearcreek's residents were foreign-born, with German and eastern European immigrants constituting a quarter of the immigrant population. Much like Butte and Anaconda, Bearcreek was a polyglot of different nationalities and ethnicities. Siegfriedt told newspaper reporters that his motto was, "Speak English, and you won't be misunderstood." A dictum he intended to impose on the Germans in Berlin. Siegfriedt's time in the military was cut short; the army discharged him in December 1918 after only two months of service. By then, though, highway commission engineer Thomas Hatcher had staked an alignment for the Black and White Trail from Bearcreek to the summit of Mount Maurice south of Red Lodge. Photographs of the survey crew taken in 1918 indicate that fishing the Beartooth's many trout-rich streams was a favorite off-hour activity for the men.

The highway commission obtained approval from the Department of Agriculture to extend the Black and White Trail to the Beartooth Plateau. It was one of twelve projects undertaken by the highway commission in the summer of 1919. The commission advertised for bids to grade, drain and construct a gravel-surfaced road with bridges and concrete culverts on 2.69 miles of the trail between Bearcreek and Red Lodge in April 1919. The highway and county commissioners opened proposals for the project in Helena in mid-May and awarded it to Columbus, Montana contractor Albert Carlson for his low bid of $29,261. Federal Aid Project no. 3 was the first project awarded to a road contractor by the State Highway Commission.

Carlson's work crews labored hard on the project during the summer of 1919. The extension branched off the Red Lodge–Bearcreek State Highway at the mouth of Scotch Coulee and then wound its way up thirteen switchbacks to the seven-thousand-foot-high level of the east side of Mount Maurice. Carlson had completed most of the work by late August that year. Only finishing touches to the grade and bridges remained. When completed, Beartooth National Forest supervisor R.T. Ferguson called the road "a wonderful piece of engineering work and has been accomplished by no less efficient a man than [Thomas] Hatcher, who engineered it from the beginning."

Doc Siegfriedt mistakenly believed it would be comparatively simple to build the next leg of the road, which would take the road up to the top of the plateau and then thirteen miles to the southwest extremity of it. Another ten miles were left to reach Beartooth Lake and the final section, a twenty-five-mile drop to Cooke City. The entire length of the planned trail extension was fifty-three miles. Siegfriedt believed the money to build the road could be raised through public subscription and government funds. The next phase of the project would occur entirely within the Beartooth National Forest. The problem, as it turned out for the physician, was to convince the Bureau of Public Roads to support the project.

Siegfriedt immediately began fundraising efforts. He raised $700 at a meeting of the Black and White Trail Association in Bearcreek in March 1920. He was even able to get Bearcreek coal miners to pledge their spare time to work on the road "at reasonable wages." In December 1920, he spoke to a meeting of the Helena Rotary Club. The *Helena Independent* described the doctor as a "physician and surgeon, mayor of Bear Creek [*sic*], coal mine manager, good fellow and Good Roads booster from away back in the hills." Siegfriedt told the audience, "I tell you Montana has the best scenery in the world. I've stated to those who talk about the Matterhorn of Switzerland that we could toss it into one of coulees down in Carbon County and lose it." Siegfriedt falsely claimed that popular subscription had paid for the completed section of the highway and that the government would finish the road (not yet confirmed). The Rotarians got caught up in the physician's enthusiasm for the trail. Rotarian songwriter Horace Ensign wrote "The Black and White Trail (the Religion of Siegfriedt)" to the tune of "A Long, Long Trail."

There's a Black and White Trail a winding
Into the land of my dreams,
Over the jagged mountains
Where the "Bear Tooth" gleams
I'll be fighting, fighting, fighting
Until my dreams come true—
'Til the day when I'll be going
From
Bearcreek to Cooke City with
You.

Even with Siegfriedt's campaigning and the enthusiastic crowds, government support for the completion of the Black and White Trail waned. The remaining fifty-three miles of the road would cross the rugged Beartooth National Forest. The rules for road-building on national forest land were different than the rules for building state roads, especially after the passage of the second Federal Aid Highway Act in 1921. The legislation that created the Forest Highway Program allocated a portion of Montana's highway apportionment for use on federal lands. The State Highway Commission and the Bureau of Public Roads allocated no funds to the Black and White Trail in 1921 or thereafter. The project had clearly run out of steam; it was too expensive and didn't provide any connectivity to other federal aid highways.

It was not until 1925 that Siegfriedt and a new partner, *Carbon County News* publisher O.H.P. Shelley, launched a campaign to build a trans-Beartooth highway on a new alignment south of Red Lodge. They were able to enlist the support of the National Park Service and Montana's powerful congressional delegation for the project. Through their efforts, President Herbert Hoover signed the Park Approach Act in 1931. Five years later, in 1936, the Bureau of Public Roads opened the Beartooth Highway to the public.

No doubt, Doc Siegfriedt was a character. A shameless promoter and amateur paleontologist, Siegfriedt didn't let the grass grow under his well-worn shoes after the failure of the Black and White Trail. In 1926, he discovered a fossil tooth in the Eagle Mine east of Bearcreek. Even before a Princeton paleontologist positively identified the fossil, Siegfriedt claimed it was of human origin, proof that Carbon County was the cradle of mankind and the Garden of Eden. In fact, the tooth belonged to an Eocene herbivore that lived 60 million years ago. Undeterred, Siegfriedt continued

The thirteen switchbacks of the Black and White Trail foreshadowed the highway up the side of the Beartooth Mountains fifteen years later. *Carbon County Historical Society, Red Lodge.*

his promotional efforts. In 1937, voters elected him mayor of Red Lodge. His promotional schemes continued unabated. The physician died of a heart attack, hat in hand, while on his way to a meeting in Red Lodge in December 1940. Today, if you look closely, you can still see the Black and White Trail climbing up the side of Mount Maurice, a monument to a failed dream.

ANCIENT LANDSCAPES

BEAVERHEAD ROCK

Perhaps one of the most well-known geological features in Montana, Beaverhead Rock, is a landmark located on Montana Highway 41, about sixteen miles northeast of Dillon. On the afternoon of August 8, 1805, members of the Lewis and Clark Expedition pulled its canoes up the Beaverhead River toward the Continental Divide. They sighted what Clark later called a "remarkable Clift" to the southwest. Sacajawea recognized this large promontory and told the captains that her people called it "beaver's head."

Beaverhead Rock is composed principally of Madison limestone. About 350 million years ago, a shallow sea covered much of Montana. Billions of tiny marine creatures thrived in the water, and when they died, their bodies settled into the muck on the seabed. After about 10 million years of accumulation and many more millions of years of compaction, this muck became the pale gray rocks that are known today as Madison limestone. This limestone is common throughout Montana, eastern Idaho, northern Wyoming and in the Dakotas. In Montana, the limestone beds range from one thousand to two thousand feet thick. Because, in Montana's dry climate, Madison limestone resists weathering and erosion much better than most other kinds of rocks, it forms many of the spectacular cliffs and ridges that make the state so scenic.

Beaverhead Rock served as an important landmark not only for Lewis and Clark but also for the trappers, miners and traders who followed them into this area. It was known to many of them as Point of Rocks. In 1863, a man named Goetschius built a stage station on the "well-traveled, deep rutted road" between Bannack and Alder Gulch

Composed of Madison limestone formed millions of years ago, Beaverhead Rock provided a dramatic setting for the Point of Rocks Stage Station in the 1860s. *MHS Photograph Archives, Helena, 952-891.*

near Beaverhead Rock. It was part of the Montana-Utah Road but was also known as Road Agents Trail because of all the robberies that occurred along it in the early 1860s. In addition to serving as a location for changing tired horses for fresh animals for the stagecoaches, the station also served meals and provided a place to sleep for stagecoach travelers. You can still see remnants of the old road, Montana Territory's most important supply route, at the base of the bluffs on the west side of the highway, within sight of Beaverhead Rock.

11

THE LONG, LONG TRAIL

The Theodore Roosevelt International Highway

The Montana Historical Society has in its voluminous collections a pamphlet that promoted and described the state's longest highway, U.S. Highway 2. Published in 1921, the Theodore Roosevelt International Highway's *Guide to Montana* is one of the few such pamphlets about Montana's early roads that survives. Brochures, like this one, were published by the many trail associations that were active in the United States in the late 1910s and 1920s. The associations intended the publications to inform motorists about trail conditions, advertise businesses and services along the route and provide information about the attractions the trail had to offer. The *Guide to Montana* is, perhaps, the most comprehensive and best illustrated of the old trail guides.

Comprising 628 miles of roadway in Montana, the Roosevelt Highway paralleled James J. Hill's Great Northern Railway along what is popularly known as the "High Line." Promoters ballyhooed the 4,060-mile-long international route as "the most wonderful Highway in all America." In reality, it was a series of interconnected county roads that became a nightmare of gumbo mud when wet, choked by dust in the dry months and impassable in the winter. None of the route in Montana was paved until the 1930s. In fact, it, at first, didn't completely cross the state. There was a 58-mile-long gap in the trail between Glacier Park Station (now East Glacier) over Marias Pass to Belton at the southern tip of Glacier National Park. Motorists had to load their automobiles onto Great Northern flatcars and ride a railroad passenger car between the two communities. It wasn't until 1930 that the Bureau of Public Roads completed the highway.

Good Roads advocates in Duluth, Minnesota, created the Theodore Roosevelt International Highway (TRIH) Association in January 1919, a few days after the death of the United States' twenty-sixth president. A vocal early Good Roads supporter, Roosevelt once stated, "It goes without saying that I appreciate the value of highways. Fundamentally they are the basis on land of the great network of trade routes which go to make up civilization." The highway, which was really more of a trail than a highway, spanned the United States through twelve states and one Canadian province between Portland, Maine, and Portland, Oregon.

The trail association established a Montana Division in late 1919. The TRIH passed through ten Montana counties and fifty-eight Montana communities. Association members along the route served as division officers. Its first president was Lyman E. Jones, the Valley County treasurer and chairman of Glasgow's chamber of commerce. In 1921, the division published its first trail guide. The association intended to publish a guide on a yearly basis or when there had been substantial changes to the road. Edited by *Glasgow Courier* editor George C. Reeder, the ninety-six-page pamphlet sports a colorful cover and a plethora of illustrations inside. The four-by-ten-inch format of the guide meant that it would fit nicely within automobile glove compartments. The TRIH entered Montana from North Dakota at the now-vanished community of Mondak and exited at Fortine near the Idaho border. The pamphlet stated that it was "published by the Montana Division solely for the benefit and use of the ever-increasing number of motorists who travel across, or partly across, this great new northern empire."

The brochure provides short descriptions of road conditions between each community on the High Line. For example, the route for 141 miles between Coberg in Blaine County and Lothair in Liberty County was in generally good condition, as it had been improved or partially improved under the auspices of the counties and the state highway commission. Other sections, however, were not so great. The segment between Brockton and Poplar in Roosevelt County had an improved dirt surface but was bad in wet weather because of gumbo. The guide describes the Roosevelt Highway from Stryker to the Idaho border as "improved, balanced rough mountain road in timber."

The pamphlet provides a short summary of each major community in each county along the trail. The agricultural opportunities offered by the Milk River Project in northeast Montana count for a lot in the booklet.

Published by the Montana Division of the Theodore Roosevelt International Highway Association, the guidebook was one of many distributed by trail associations in Montana. *MDT.*

Hunting and fishing pervade the guide in western Montana. Also noted in the guide are "above average hotels," tourist camps, garages, automobile dealerships, banks and other businesses along the route. Perhaps not surprising is the attention paid to Glacier National Park as a destination. Road conditions are, again, described along with the rules for automobiles in the national park. Potential tourists were directed that "careful driving is required at all times"; muffler "cutouts" must be closed when passing horses,

The Roosevelt Highway was a mixture of very good and very bad road conditions. In Lincoln County, the road was mostly "improved." *MDT.*

hotels and campgrounds; and cars must be equipped with good brakes, horns and lights. Importantly, "Teams have the right-of-way at all times and in all places. If horses appear nervous, automobiles will take the outer edge of the road and engine will be stopped until horses have passed." The guide was careful to note that these were not regulations but strong suggestions.

In 1926, the Federal Bureau of Public Roads and the American Association of State Highway Officials gave the road its current numerical designation, U.S. Highway 2. They also changed the western terminus of the highway from Portland, Oregon, to Everett, Washington. In Montana, the State Highway Commission began an ambitious program to improve and pave the highway during the 1930s. The commission continued to refer to it as the Roosevelt Highway until 1939. The TRIH Association remained active until at least 1939, with unsuccessful attempts to continue its efforts afterward. It seems World War II permanently ended the association's efforts to promote the "most wonderful highway in all America."

Yet even today, Glasgow bank president and trail promoter Harry B. Tyson's words echo about the highway, "To you travelers of the 'long, long trail' Montana opens her magnificent distances to you. When on the great plains, or high in the mighty Rockies, breath [*sic*] deep of this pure out door. Let the spirit of the great spaces fill you, and remember you are out where the west begins."

12

THE MOST PICTURESQUE HIGHWAY IN THE WEST

Harding Way

With the dawn of the automobile age in Montana, a good road over Pipestone Pass to Butte took on new significance. A road had existed over the pass since at least the 1870s, but it was hardly adequate for automobiles in the early twentieth century. The city's political, business and civic leaders recognized early on the need for a better road over the Continental Divide but were hampered by the lack of funding. There were no state or federal funds available for road improvements, and the county couldn't foot the whole bill for the work. Consequently, in 1911, Butte First National Bank president Andrew J. Davis spent $20,000 of his personal fortune to "put in such condition that autos can now climb what was formerly the hardest piece of mountain road in the state." Fêted at a banquet at the Silver Bow Club in December 1911, Davis acknowledged to the hundred or so attendees that Montana laws regarding roads were fine but that those in office were indifferent to them. After presenting Davis with a "handsome silver loving cup," the assembled crowd organized the Butte Automobile Club, elected Davis president and named the improved section of road Davis Grade in his honor.

In 1914, the Montana State Highway Commission designated the old road from Butte across Pipestone Pass to Whitehall a part of the state highway system, which made it eligible for federal funds for improvements, should they become available. The designation coincided with the Yellowstone Trail Association's extension of the highway to the West Coast from Livingston. In 1916, Congress enacted the first Federal Aid Highway

Act to provide money on a matching basis to the states. The money could be used only by the states on the Federal Aid Highway System. Because the counties provided the matching funds, they dictated to the highway commission which projects would be funded. It was not until 1917, when the legislature reorganized the highway commission, that it began to expend federal funds on Montana's highways.

Little more than a wagon trail, the old road was clearly a challenge to motorists during the first two decades of the twentieth century. One pundit described driving the road as feeling "akin to sliding off the roof of a high peaked building." The treacherous road was one of the most dangerous on the entire 3,719-mile length of the Yellowstone Trail. Motorists, after crossing the pass from the east, initially found the descent a relatively easy 6 percent grade. But it soon increased to 20 percent. A car's speed would increase to the point that it wouldn't allow a driver to stop or change gears—they were dependent on brakes alone and prayed they would hold. The curves, lack of guardrails and other dangers associated with a primitive mountain road made what was called in Butte Eighteen-Mile Hill perilous in all conditions.

In April 1921, State Highway Commission chairman George W. Lanstrum announced to the press a project to improve the Yellowstone Trail on Eighteen-Mile Hill. Lanstrum intended the ambitious project to reduce many of the road's steep grades and install guardrails to prevent motorists from hurtling over the edge of the roadway. The project would put to work Butte men who had lost their employment due to a labor strike against the Anaconda Copper Mining Company. The Silver Bow County commissioners, headed by Joseph M. Fabian, promoted Lanstrum's plan and agreed to pay half the cost of the project. By the following month, Montana Highway Department chief engineer John Edy announced to the press that the project would start in a couple weeks, even though the plans for the highway were nowhere near completed.

Potential laborers on the project registered for the project in late June before the highway plans were ready. The county, not the contractor, was responsible for hiring the work crew. Nearly one thousand unemployed men applied for the one hundred jobs available for the project. Because there would be significant blasting on the project, applications for miners with experience handling explosives received preferential consideration by the county. Silver Bow County surveyor Michael Loughran supervised the work along with a Montana Highway Department engineer. Evidence suggests that the county had hired the crew by early July 1921, but it would be nearly two months before work would begin on the Eighteen-Mile Hill project.

Once the state had completed the road plans and secured the federal funding for the project, the highway and county commissions moved forward to let the project out to contract. Both commissions specified each contractor submit two bids for the project: one under the prevailing Butte union wage scale and the other based on an unrestricted scale. Twelve contractors submitted bids for the project, which ranged from $73,953 to $194,768 under the union scale to $87,822 to $111,342 under the unrestricted scale. When the commissions opened the bids on August 5, 1921, they argued over which wage scale to accept. That delayed letting the contract. The debate about the wage scale continued between the county commissioners, contractors and highway commissioners for several days as the 1921 construction season faded. The *Butte Miner* lamented, "A certain unmentionable place is said to be paved with good intentions. It begins to look as though that might be the kind of paving which the Eighteen-Mile Hill will be laid." Eventually, the county commissioners prevailed and accepted the union wage scale. On August 12, the two commissions awarded the project to the Heiselt Construction Company of Salt Lake City. The contractor began work on the project five days later.

By mid-September, the project was well underway. Heiselt worked its crews from both ends of the 2.43-mile-long project. Along with the blasting, the contractor utilized a steam shovel and "as many men as can be employed to advantage." Crews built stone retaining walls along the route and installed thirteen sections of heavy log guardrails between the edge of the road and the precipice. Of the twenty-one culverts laid on the project, two were concrete box culverts located on the switchback section of the roadway. Heiselt, though, was in a race against winter to complete as much of the project as possible before snow closed the project down. The company didn't make it. Heiselt obtained an extension on the project to the spring of 1922.

By April, the contractor had still not completed the project. The county commissioners toured the road that month and noted the presence of overhanging boulders, "which do not promise well for safety." Heiselt surfaced the twenty-one-foot-wide roadway with decomposed granite acquired from sources on the pass. It was, according to the *Jefferson Valley News*, smooth as a "new-laid boulevard." Although the road was incomplete, its contractor officially opened it to automobile traffic on July 4, 1922. Heiselt finished up the project later in the month. The highway commission's 1921–22 biennial report crowed about the project "said by many to be the best road in the state."

By all accounts, President Warren G. Harding was "pleased" when Butte citizens named the new highway in his honor. *Library of Congress.*

Even before the highway was open for traffic, the county commissioners and local civic groups made plans to name it. From 1913 to 1926, Montana was crisscrossed by named highways, such as the Roosevelt Highway, Vigilante Trail and Custer Battlefield Highway. These named roads provided connections between the state's national parks, historic sites and other tourist attractions. The segment under construction was part of the Yellowstone Trail, but Butte and county leaders wanted to customize the highway to draw more traffic to it. "[After] what is alleged to have been a nerve-wrecking, sleep-banishing struggle with a long list of proposed designations," the county commissioners finally decided to name the new highway Harding Way, after U.S. president Warren G. Harding. The president pronounced himself pleased with the honor in a letter to the county commissioners the following month.

From the beginning, many in Butte perceived Harding Way as more than just a connection between the city and Whitehall. They envisioned the road as a playground for Butte residents and as a scenic gateway to the Mining City. The Butte Chamber of Commerce hyped the road as a destination point for Mining City "Sunday" drivers and a scenic route for tourists. The highway bisected Thompson Park, a 3,300-acre municipal park dedicated to the city by mining engineer William Boyce Thompson in 1915 and expanded by the Beaverhead-Deerlodge National Forest in 1922. In the 1920s and 1930s, the park included hiking trails, scenic roads and other facilities that provided

Warren G. Harding on a visit to Helena. *Library of Congress.*

Butte citizens with a pastoral escape from life in what many considered the ugliest city in the United States.

In August 1922, Butte plumbers William Magill and Charles Nevin obtained the county commissioners' permission to install a water fountain at the switchback section of the highway. The porcelain fountain was to be equipped with a hose to fill thirsty automobile radiators. It was also to include a bubbler for people, a horse trough and a "private fount" for dogs. It wasn't until June 1923, however, that Magill and Nevin installed the fountain.

Just four years later, the Butte Kiwanis Club made plans to replace the old fountain with a new architect-designed concrete fountain across the highway from the old fountain. The civic club obtained permission from the county commissioners to erect the memorial fountain, which was to be fed by a spring and include two bubblers. At the end of July 1927, a crew under the supervision of Anaconda Company salesman Ray Gill and Butte contractor Michael O'Connell poured the concrete and installed the plumbing fixtures for the fountain. Butte architect Walter Arnold designed the memorial fountain. Just a few hours after they completed the fountain, however, vandals significantly damaged it by throwing rocks at the wet concrete and grinding their heels into it. They also "shoved a big boulder into the bowl of the fountain." By mid-August, the Kiwanis Club had repaired the fountain and attached a bronze tablet on the feature that read, "Greetings Thirsty Wayfarer. Butte Kiwanis Club 1927."

In 1926, the Federal Bureau of Public Roads (BPR), the American Association of State Highway Officials (AASHO) and the state highway commission enacted a highway numbering system to replace the named highways that proliferated across the United States. The BPR and AASHO intended to bring order to the chaos of highways in the United States. Accordingly, the Yellowstone Trail, which spanned the country from Plymouth, Massachusetts, to Puget Sound became U.S. Highway 10. In Montana, U.S. 10 split at Three Forks with branches running north through Helena and south through Butte. They rejoined at Garrison, Montana. The Butte branch was U.S. Highway 10–South.

Traffic on Harding Way steadily increased in the late 1920s. In October 1929, the highway commission programmed a project to reconstruct several dangerous curves on the roadway. The proposed project included widening the roadway to twenty-four feet in addition to eliminating the dangerous curves. On February 26, 1930, the highway commission awarded a project

A classic early twentieth-century mountain highway, Harding Way offered provided economic and recreational benefits to Butte's citizens. *Butte–Silver Bow Archives.*

to Butte contractor Leo T. Lawler to regrade, widen and straighten 2.25 miles of the Harding Way section of U.S. Highway 10–South.

Lawler began work on the project in April 1930. By early May, the project was far enough along that Montana Highway Department division engineer Edward B. Donahue asked motorists, especially Sunday drivers, to avoid sightseeing on Harding Way north of the Kiwanis Club fountain. Vehicles, he said, slowed the work down and lengthened the construction time. By mid-May, the highway department and contractor had closed the highway down while construction continued and detoured traffic onto the old road south of Butte. Lawler worked two shifts on the project and made steady enough progress on it that the route was reopened on June 14. An article that appeared in the *Montana Standard* in June stated that "improvements on the scenic road are nearly complete" and that it would soon be ready for the expected heavy tourist traffic that summer.

Congress allotted a portion of Montana's federal aid allocation for use on federally owned land, such as national forests. In May 1930, the BPR and Montana highway commissioners met in Helena to earmark funds for use by the BPR. They chose ten projects, including the section of U.S. Highway 10–South within the Beaverhead-Deerlodge National Forest. In July 1930, BPR surveyor Birney Kitt staked a route for U.S. Highway 10–South for a new highway east of the Pipestone Pass summit. By the following month, the BPR was deep into developing the plans for 3.3 miles of roadway. By early October, the BPR had advertised for bids to construct the route. The BPR opened bids for its Pipestone Pass project on October 21. Once again, Leo Lawler was the successful bidder.

Outside the national forest, the highway was under the jurisdiction of the Montana State Highway Commission. In January 1931, highway department engineers surveyed U.S. Highway 10–South outside the Forest Highway project east toward Whitehall. The commission awarded the project to Spokane contractor James Crick to construct 14.5 miles of the Whitehall–Pipestone Pass section of U.S. 10–South in July that year. Crick's crews labored on the project, straightening curves and lowering the grade, through the remainder of 1931, completing the project in May 1932. The new highway reduced the mileage between Butte and Whitehall by several miles.

Granite boulders near the top of Pipestone Pass provided a unique opportunity for Butte businesses to advertise their services to travelers on the highway. There are five painted rock billboards on the Jefferson County side of the pass and two rock billboards in Silver Bow County.

An unknown Butte sign painter painted the signs on the rocks sometime between 1931 and 1934.

Loiselle Taxi Service advertised prominently on three of the painted boulders on the Jefferson and Silver Bow sides of the county line. Born in Basin, Montana, in 1892, Alex Loiselle worked as a chauffeur in Butte beginning around 1912. Driving a Cadillac limousine, he formed the Loiselle Taxi Service in June 1921. The company ceased operations about 1934. That year, he became a private limousine driver for Howard Pierce and others until his death in an automobile accident near Lovelock, Nevada, on March 21, 1936. Loiselle likely had the advertising signs painted on the rocks shortly after the completion of the 1931 highway project.

Alex Loiselle may have played another role in a dark chapter of Butte's history. Historians Will Roscoe and Jane Little Botkin have implicated Loiselle in the murder of Industrial Workers of the World (IWW) labor organizer Frank Little in 1917. There were few Cadillacs in Butte in 1917. Loiselle drove one, as did some Anaconda Company executives. Early in

Harding Way is carved through the rocky Boulder batholith landscape. Granite outcrops, like this one, provided photograph opportunities for motorists. *Smithers Photograph, MDT.*

the morning of August 1, 1917, six men entered a boardinghouse on North Wyoming Street, dragged Little out, still in his underwear, and hustled him into the back of a Cadillac. After dragging Little behind the car through uptown Butte, the men drove the labor organizer to the southern outskirts of town, where they hanged him from a Milwaukee Road trestle. A teamster found Little shortly after daybreak. Some historians implicated Loiselle as the one who drove the Cadillac. He had recently purchased the car from Howard Pierce, who later died in the same car accident as Loiselle in 1936.

Other than routine maintenance and replacing the original guardrails, there have been no substantial changes to Harding Way since the completion of its last construction project in 1934. In 1966, the Montana Highway Department completed construction of the Homestake Pass section of Interstate 90 between Whitehall and Butte. When completed, the primary highway route over the Continental Divide east of Butte shifted from Harding Way to Homestake Pass. Harding Way retained its title of U.S. Highway 10–South until 1987, when the state highway commission redesignated it Montana Highway 2. Today, Harding Way provides motorists with a taste of what highways were like in the early twentieth century. One constant between the highway in 1934 and today is that one needs to keep both eyes on the road and both hands on the steering wheel—and, of course, wear your seatbelt.

13

MONTANA'S WONDER ROAD

The Skalkaho Road

It is comparatively seldom that any highway organization has an opportunity to survey and build a road in practically virgin territory—thru places where the foot of man has never tread.
—Montana Highway News, *November 1922*

The Roaring Twenties was an era of substantial road construction efforts by federal, state and local governments as Montana moved headlong into the automobile age. All roads were intended to provide better connections between the state's metropolitan areas, improve the state's economy and provide residents and tourists opportunities to enjoy Montana's picturesque marvels. State and local promoters, for example, intended the Black and White Trail in Carbon County to open a new entrance to Yellowstone National Park and give mining trucks in the Cooke City area an outlet to the railroad in Red Lodge. Harding Way in Silver Bow County and the Jefferson River Canyon in Jefferson County are other examples of practical routes that offered spectacular scenery as an incentive for travelers. One road figures prominently in the state's road-building efforts in Montana during the decade: the Skalkaho Road in Ravalli and Granite Counties.

The Skalkaho Trail was used by the region's Native people for generations before Euro-Americans arrived in the Bitterroot valley in the 1840s. In Salish, *skalkaho* means either "place of the beaver" or "many trails." Road-builder John Mullan mentioned a place called "Sharkahole" in his 1863 congressional report. Surveyor Walter DeLacey noted it on his

1865 map of Montana Territory as "Ska-Ka-Ke." Early upper Bitterroot residents referred to it by its Native name. Farmers began settling along Skalkaho Creek in the 1860s. In 1868, three men, Robert Pringle, Robert Simpson and Joshua Reed, petitioned the territorial legislature to license the Bitterroot and Philipsburg Wagon Road. Their efforts failed to succeed. In 1872, however, an unknown man established a small settlement on Skalkaho Creek and managed to acquire a post office for a short time.

In the late nineteenth century, copper king Marcus Daly envisioned a railroad between the upper Bitterroot valley and his smelter town of Anaconda. Daly even went as far as to survey for the extension of his Butte, Anaconda and Pacific Railroad from Anaconda to Hamilton. His death in 1900, however, ended any plans to extend the railroad to the Bitterroot. Even though Daly's plan didn't pan out, boosters soon began pushing for the construction of a road between the Bitterroot and Philipsburg at the turn of the twentieth century. Hamilton dentist and outdoorsman Robert W. Beck and other Good Roads enthusiasts scouted the Skalkaho Trail and Skalkaho Falls. Dr. Beck "and his fellow trail-loving Hamiltonians smoked many a pipe planning and hoping their pipe dreams would be someday fulfilled." It was mainly through the efforts of Beck's and others that the pipe dreams eventually saw fruition.

Momentum from Bitterroot valley citizens for the road increased in the mid-1910s and culminated in September 1921, when the State Highway Commission awarded a project to Clifton, Applegate and Toole (CAT) of Spokane to construct a little over fifteen miles of roadway between Hamilton and Philipsburg. Half of the money for the project came from the federal government, and half came from a bond election approved by Ravalli County voters in April 1920. Prior to the project letting, the highway commission designated the proposed route a state highway. The state highway department's Missoula district engineer and his crew surveyed the proposed route of the Skalkaho Road on the Ravalli County side of the divide from May to September 1921. Bureau of Public Roads engineer Howard J. Taylor surveyed the Granite County side of the mountains. Newspaper accounts suggest the surveyors mostly followed an existing pack trail.

The Spokane contractor began work on the project a few days after winning the contract. The highway commission appointed Frank Monty as the resident engineer to oversee the construction of the road. Leo Lawler acted as the contractor's supervisor. The project proved daunting for CAT. The contractor maintained a work crew of around fifty men, many of

Despite contemporary newspapers touting it as a modern highway, Skalkaho Road was little more than an improved dirt track through a dense forest. *MDT.*

whom were Serbians and Finns brought in from Butte. The crew lived in eight camps strung along the route. The project required considerable blasting and the construction of hairpin curves and numerous turnouts. The highway engineers designed a grade of no more than 5 percent as the road climbed nearly three thousand feet from the western base to the summit of the Sapphire Mountains at Skalkaho Pass.

On fill sections more than six feet deep, the workers installed nearly forty-five thousand linear feet of log guardrail or stone blocks to keep traffic on the narrow winding road. Skalkaho Road included eighty-seven log culverts and nine log bridges. Limited funds meant the road could be no more than fourteen feet wide. Although CAT employed a steam shovel on the project, most was pick and shovel work; the crews relied heavily on horses to pull graders and other equipment. The work was slow, much too slow for people in the Bitterroot valley. After two years, in 1923, the road was still not completed. The *Hamilton Western News* lamented that "the inertia which has caused the road to remain uncompleted is wasteful, foolhardy, and incomprehensible."

Indeed, the project had more than its fair share of problems. Just a couple weeks after the highway commission awarded the project to CAT, the first of many change orders from the Montana Highway Department arrived on the contractor's desk. Resident engineer Monty and other highway department engineers continually made changes in the alignment of the road, the amount of soil excavated and other modifications to the design. Changes in orders would prove a plague to CAT as it watched its profit margin dwindle and eventually go into the red. Importantly, because of the changed orders, the deadline for the completion of the project became meaningless. The contractor submitted claim after claim for contract adjustments to the highway commission, which often decided not to consider them "based on alleged construction costs." While the highway commission believed many of CAT's claims were questionable, the contractor argued that the commission's engineers were incompetent. CAT's claims continued through the duration of the project and eventually resulted in litigation long after the completion of the road. Ultimately, the commission and CAT settled the issue out of court four years after CAT completed the project. Other problems included labor shortages, bad weather, a labor strike for higher wages, injuries sustained by workers and the death of a man from a rock fall in August 1922.

Under the provisions of the 1921 Federal Highway Act, the segment of the highway located within the Bitterroot National Forest fell under different

The completion of Skalkaho Road in 1924 made what was originally called Beck Falls, a spectacular cascade in Ravalli County, accessible to motorists. *Author's collection.*

construction rules and a different contractor. Instead, the Federal Bureau of Public Roads (BPR) designed and built the road because it was within the Bitterroot National Forest. In May 1922, the BPR let a contract to Great Falls contractor White, Brown and Leahy to build the road within the national forest. Unlike on the contractors on the Ravalli County side of the mountains, the BPR and contractor worked well together without the squabbling that characterized the relationship between the state highway commission and CAT. The contractor completed the Granite County segment of the Skalkaho Road in October 1923.

By the spring of 1924, the Skalkaho Road project finally neared completion. As was common in those days, the people who would benefit most from the road planned to celebrate the opening of the road. In mid-June, three hundred automobiles from Missoula, Hamilton and Anaconda formed an autocade to navigate the new road. With banners decorating the sides of the cars, the caravan arrived in Butte late in the day, and its members were treated to a banquet at the Hotel Finlen by the Butte Chamber of Commerce. The *Western News* claimed the route was lined with automobiles full of picnic parties along its length. The road's official opening occurred on July 20, 1924. That day, celebrants from both sides of the mountains met at an unspecified location, feasted on barbecued beef and listened to speakers extol the wonders of the "America's most beautiful scenic highway" and how it would draw Montanans closer together. Attendees at the gala enjoyed live music, dancing and singing among other activities. The celebration's sponsors provided the celebrants "thousands of donuts, loaves of bread, and barrels of coffee."

The story of the Skalkaho Road didn't end with the 1924 opening. The route officially attained federal aid status as Montana Highway 38 in 1931. The Bitterroot National Forest later christened it the Skalkaho Highway Scenic Byway. Although Skalkaho Road is closed in the winters, the Montana Department of Transportation regularly maintains it. Its historic appearance remains, as does the thrill of crossing the Sapphire Mountains and visiting Skalkaho Falls on one of Montana's most scenic and least visited historic highways.

14

MUNDANE YET SIGNIFICANT

Montana's Timber Bridges

P robably the least interesting bridge type is among the most important for the development of Montana's highways. Timber bridges enabled the fantastic expansion of the highway system during the Great Depression. There are, however, no tales of remarkable engineering feats associated with them or any juicy stories involving their construction. They remain the most common bridge type on Montana's highways. These bridges are structurally unremarkable. Bridge engineers designed them to be uncomplicated and inexpensive to build so that contractors could build a lot of them to keep up with the highway programs. Currently, Montana has over 1,600 bridges on its National Highway System's primary, secondary, urban and other routes. Approximately 20 percent of them are timber bridges mostly located in central and eastern Montana. They may be so important because they are so unexceptional.

Timber bridges consist of precut and creosote-treated components and could be constructed easily across small streams, drainages and coulee crossings. They range in length from 20 to 380 feet; the average span is 19 feet. Multi-span structures rest on timber piling bents, some with diagonal sway braces and a few with the pilings encased in wood plank walls. The decks are supported by 6-by-18-inch timber beams, called stringers, with 2-by-4-inch wood decks overlayed with either asphalt or gravel on the state's more isolated rural roads; timber curbs with sheet metal drains delineate the roadway. The number of stringers depended on the width and length of the structure. Originally, motorists could easily recognize timber bridges by the double-rowed wood guardrails that were often painted white and flanked the deck. Today, there are few timber bridges with their original guardrails. Beginning in the 1970s, the MDT removed the top rails or completely replaced them with steel guardrails. This allowed the structures to accommodate wider loads, especially in the agricultural areas of the state. The original specifications also stipulated that Douglas fir trees, which are grown in the wetter climate of the Pacific Northwest, would be best suited for these timber bridges.

The Montana State Highway Commission's first bridge engineer, Charles Kyle, developed a standardized timber bridge design in the summer of 1915. The commission utilized that design, with modifications based on changing traffic demands, until the early 1960s and the beginning of the interstate highway era. Sheridan County built the first highway commission–designed timber bridge on an unnamed route in the fall of 1915. Big Horn County built the second timber bridge around the same time. It crossed Fly Creek a little over three miles from the community of Toluca. Both were two-span structures with pile bents and the familiar double-rowed wood guardrails. Hundreds of timber bridges followed them on Montana's highways. As it turned out, timber bridges were perfect for the highway building booms of the late 1920s and 1930s.

Timber bridges grew in importance in the development of the highway system after the passage of Montana's Good Roads Law in November 1927. The law enacted a three-cents-per-gallon gasoline tax that provided the highway commission with the matching money needed to qualify for federal highway funds. From 1928 until 1930, commission contractors built 241 timber bridges on Montana's Federal Aid Primary Highway System. The design deviated little from the design developed by Charles Kyle in 1915, with one important addition: new specifications for timber bridges mandated the timber components be treated with a preservative, creosote, to make them more long-lasting and durable. Wood preserving companies in Oregon and Washington supplied creosote-treated bridge components to Montana contractors well into the 1950s. By 1930, the number of timber bridges exceeded the number of steel truss, reinforced concrete and steel stringer bridges built on the state's highways.

Even though Montana's economy tanked during the Great Depression, road and bridge construction boomed during that decade. From January 1931 to December 1941, the Montana Highway Department built 1,145 bridges on the state's primary and secondary roads. Of those, 948, or 83 percent, were timber bridges. The highway department built most timber

Timber bridges were practical ways to cross small streams and coulees. Pictured is White Bear Creek Bridge on U.S. 2, west of Dodson in 1924. *MDT.*

bridges in eastern Montana, where the drier climate functioned as a natural preservative that augmented the creosote-treated structural components. Indeed, most of the existing Great Depression–era timber bridges that still carry traffic are located in eastern Montana. Like the steel truss bridges, there were a few contractors who specialized in the construction of timber bridges; they included Walter Mackin of Billings, Dave Manning of Hysham and Leroy Lockwood of Glasgow.

After three years of minimal operations during World War II, the highway commission initiated a second highway construction boom in the postwar years. The commission, however, built fewer timber bridges and concentrated more on prestressed concrete, steel stringer and steel girder structures. The highway commission contracted for the construction of only 211 timber bridges from 1945 to 1960, most of them on secondary highways. Changes to the design primarily involved the addition of extra stringers to accommodate the heavier traffic loads and the loss of the top rails of the guardrails.

Timber bridges are still abundant on Montana's transportation landscape. Unlike many other states, which relied more on steel stringer and reinforced concrete bridges to expeditiously span obstacles, Montana, with its arid climate, which proved an excellent preservative for timber bridges, has many of its timber bridges still in service. Simple in design, these bridges

The Montana Highway Department built well over one thousand timber bridges, mostly in eastern Montana, from 1928 to 1960. They all looked pretty much the same. *MDT.*

were uncomplicated, inexpensive and could be built in large numbers. They were perfect for the make-work programs of the Great Depression and expedient in the 1950s. Eventually, however, the introduction of cheaper steel and prestressed concrete had a profound impact on the number of new timber bridges. Timber bridges, however, still exist in large numbers in eastern Montana and are a testament to the hardiness of the design and the Montana Highway Department's early road-building efforts.

15

HANGING THE GOLDEN LANTERNS

Montana's Nighttime Airway Beacons

By the early 1940s, Montana was crisscrossed by a network of airway routes used by the nation's airlines for passengers, airmail and commercial purposes. Private pilots also utilized the air routes as they provided connections between airports and airfields. One critical component of the air routes was the nighttime navigational beacon. By World War II, seventy nighttime airway beacons spanned the length and width of Montana. Most paralleled the state's major highways. In the eastern two-thirds of the state, the beacon towers were spaced every ten miles, while in the mountainous west, they were located about fifteen miles apart. In between were intermediary or emergency landing fields, many of which also had beacons standing near the runways. Within a short time, the federal government also activated a radio beacon system in the state that augmented the flashing beacons. The beacons faithfully stood sentinel across Montana, guiding pilots at night and sometimes in adverse weather conditions. By the 1960s, however, they had become obsolete due to advances in radar and electronic guidance systems. Montana was the last state in the country to operate and maintain a nighttime beacon system. A few private individuals and the Idaho Aviation Heritage Foundation, however, still operate and maintain thirteen beacons in the Treasure State as a reminder of Montana's early aviation history.

In 1934, the federal government chose the pioneering air service Northwest Airlines to fly the newly established Northern Transcontinental Airway between Seattle and New York. By the time of its selection, Northwest Airlines had worked in the airmail business for several years.

Colonel Lewis Brittin founded the airline in September 1926 to fly mail for the U.S. Post Office Department in the upper Midwest. The following year, the company began carrying passengers and changed its name to Northwest Airlines. In 1929, a group of Minneapolis businessmen, headed by Richard Lilly, purchased the airline from Brittin. The new owners expanded the air fleet and the company's services into Illinois and southern Canada. By the mid-1930s, when it was selected to fly the Northern Transcontinental Airway, Northwest Airlines had twenty-three airplanes and employed over 100 people, including 23 pilots and copilots. The airline flew 5,180 miles daily and carried 17,532 passengers in 1933. By 1939, there were three daily flights between Minneapolis and Seattle with extensions into the western Pacific Ocean to Japan and Alaska.

The U.S. Department of Commerce's Bureau of Air Commerce had big plans for the Northern Transcontinental Airway. In September 1934, the bureau announced plans to construct 125 beacon lights and intermediate emergency landing fields every fifty miles on the airway route between Minneapolis-St. Paul and Seattle. The bureau estimated the cost of the project at around $275,000, all of which would be paid by the Federal Project Works Administration, a New Deal agency. Construction of the first towers in Montana began in October 1934 between Miles City and Billings.

The beacons consisted of steel towers that varied between fifty-five and ninety-one feet in height, depending on the terrain. The towers were crowned by a metal platform and pedestal that held the revolving, flashing beacon. The U.S. Department of Commerce's aeronautics branch standardized the design of the beacon towers, beacons and generator sheds by 1931. In Montana, the International Derrick and Equipment Company of Columbus, Ohio, fabricated the towers utilizing open-hearth steel with all components galvanized. Each tower weighed a little over two tons.

Also In 1931, the U.S. Patent Office granted John Bartow a patent for a new type of beacon, which combined the advantages of high candlepower "of the projector type with the wide-angle visibility of the flashing type" of beacon. The beacon, encased by a twenty-inch glass dome, solved the problem of uneven pressure from high winds and proved less liable to freeze up in inclement weather in remote locations. The dome housed a twenty-four-inch reflector amplified by three lenses, making the beacon light distinguishable from other lights. The system also included red and green directional lights that corresponded with the air route; the red course lights flashed a Morse code signal identifying the specific beacon to pilots. Bartow licensed General Electric to manufacture the beacons. The company continued to refine the design, which became the standard for beacons on the mountainous portion of the Northern Transcontinental and National Parks Airway Routes by 1934.

The Bartow Beacon emitted one million candlepower every one-tenth of a second that could easily be seen over the rugged terrain in the American West. The beacon rotated at six rotations per minute, and each beacon unit included a spare light bulb in case one should burn out. Andrew Boone wrote in 1932:

> *Seldom does a beacon light anywhere on the nation's air chain dim and die out. Two bulbs are fitted into each of the million-candle-power lights, although only one burns. Should the filament burn out, the light would dim momentarily while the other bulb is being pulled into an upright position by the electrically operated mechanism.*

The bulb reportedly could be automatically placed in position within a few seconds of the primary bulb's failure.

Electricity powered the beacons, either through a direct power line connection or by a self-starting generator in more remote locations. The buildings that accompanied these lights were constructed from a variety of locally accessible materials, the most common being wood or standing seam metal, depending on site conditions. Each building housed two generators: the primary unit and a backup should the main generator fail. These generators started and stopped running after receiving a signal from either an astronomical clock or a photocell at dusk and at dawn. In 1936, the *Montana Standard* described the astronomical clock at the Homestake Pass near Butte: "On the day the light was placed in operation, representative of the Bureau of Air Commerce wound a clock that control[led] the beacon. If not forgotten in the meantime, the clock will again be wound on December 12, 1945." Despite that, evidence suggests the photocells were best suited for "the unusual conditions caused by a cloudy or bright day."

The electrical signal initiated a start-up sequence that involved the "crank, choke, start and connect" of the engine. Each generator utilized a thirty-two-volt storage battery to begin the sequence. The operation of the generator kept the battery charged and each generator was equipped with thermostats and oil heaters in areas of severe winter weather. When the temperature dropped below forty degrees Fahrenheit, the starting sequence initiated itself. Gasoline motors fed by 515-gallon storage tanks located next to the generator house powered the generators. Each generator used nine-tenths

The Augusta airport beacon once guided air traffic on the Northern Transcontinental Airway. It originally stood at Drummond and was later moved to Augusta. *MDT.*

of a quart of white gasoline per each kilowatt hour. Ideally, the gasoline tank required filling once every eight months.

The Bureau of Air Commerce employed an army of "mechanicians" to maintain the beacon system. The men visited each beacon every two weeks and made adjustments and repairs when necessary. On average, the generators required a complete overhaul every two years. Most of the time, major repairs and generator overhauls occurred on site; moving a generator off site for repairs occurred infrequently. Maintenance duties included greasing the rotating beacons, replacing burned-out bulbs and adjusting the directional lights. Many of the beacon sites in Montana included a warming shack for the mechanicians. The shacks featured a bed, a fold-down desk, a chair and a woodstove. One of those shacks survives at the St. Regis Airway Beacon.

The Bureau of Air Commerce constructed beacons on the Lookout Pass–Bozeman Pass segment of the airway route in the spring, summer and fall of 1935. The erection of the beacon towers between Bozeman and Helena occurred in the summer of that year. By early September, beacons had been erected at Bozeman Pass, Strawberry Butte, Townsend and the Spokane Hills east of Helena. Supervised by bureau engineer A.S. Watson were construction crews comprising twenty-four men, all hired through the National Re-Employment Service offices in the counties where the construction occurred. Skilled workers and supervisors, however, were not hired through the service. The crews completed towers at Belgrade and Toston by September 15, 1935. When the bureau completed the beacon system to Helena, Northwest Airlines flew a Lockheed Electra passenger plane into the city's municipal airport the night of September 15. The inaugural flight utilized the beacons to navigate to Helena. From there, the flight turned south to Butte and then proceeded west toward Seattle.

Concurrent with the erection of the Bozeman Pass–Helena beacons, the Bureau of Air Commerce began installing twelve beacons on the Lookout Pass–MacDonald Pass segment of the Northern Transcontinental route in February 1935. The airway followed the route of the wagon road built by Captain John Mullan between 1859 and 1862. Since many of the beacons in western Montana were located in national forests, Air Commerce enlisted the aid of the National Forest Service in erecting the beacons. In late March 1935, the National Forest Service provided mule pack trains from its Nine Mile Remount Station to carry nearly fourteen thousand pounds of "steel, sand, gravel and other material" to the beacon construction site on University Mountain a few miles east of Missoula. Forest service packers and mules also hauled construction materials to other beacon sites on the Lolo National Forest in Montana.

The Bureau of Air Commerce completed its construction of the Northern Transcontinental Airway beacons in November 1935. The last beacon erected on the route between Minneapolis and Seattle stood atop MacDonald Pass, west of Helena. The Civil Aeronautics Administration (CAA) lit the beacon at a public ceremony on November 10, 1935. The completion of the system caused celebration in Helena, as attested by a November 22 event held at Helena Municipal Airport, where an estimated four thousand people braved frigid weather to attend. Attendees heard speeches by local officials, including Eugene Vidal, the director of the Bureau of Air Commerce (and father of author Gore Vidal). The *Helena Independent* called the celebration the "Hanging of the Golden Lantern marking the inauguration of the night flight of the Northwest Airlines following completion of the beacon system from the Twin Cities to the coast."

The Bureau of Air Commerce began work on lighting the Salt Lake City–Butte segment of the National Parks Airway Route simultaneously with the Northern Transcontinental Route, both of which included a Helena stop. Air commerce surveyors surveyed the Dell-Helena segment of the line in

The MacDonald Pass beacon still lights up the night sky west of Helena. It is listed in the National Register of Historic Places. *MDT*.

the summer of 1935. Work on the installation of the ten beacons between Helena and Dell in Beaverhead County began in October that year. The *Montana Standard* reported that the beacons would be located approximately fifteen miles apart with flashers installed to indicate obstructions through the mountainous country. By the first week of November, Bureau of Air Commerce crews had erected three of the five beacons between Helena and Butte, including the Homestake Beacon, which had to be installed before winter set in. Each beacon was "of the revolving type, casting a ray of more than 1,000,000 candlepower." The U.S. Department of Commerce threw the switch to light the Homestake Beacon in mid-December 1935. The *Helena Independent* reported that the beacon would "guide planes into Butte at night, a revolving beacon has been put into operation." Hadfield supervised the construction crews on the project, all of which of which were hired through the Butte and Helena National Reemployment Offices.

The Department of Commerce completed the installation of the beacons between Helena and Dell by mid-December 1935. The inaugural night flight on the National Parks Airway occurred on December 20, 1935. Late in the evening, a twin-motored Boeing airliner carrying ten passengers and mail landed at the Helena Municipal Airport. The landing was attended by a crowd of "hundreds" of Helena citizens. After photographs and refueling, the plane left for Butte. The *Montana Standard* reported:

> *Shortly after midnight the great Boeing took off again for Butte, following the beacons of Canyon Ferry, Boulder Hill, and Elk Park. Ten minutes out of Helena, Butte's multi-colored Christmas raiment of dazzling lights stood out in bold relief in the darkness ahead and shortly after the National Parks' first official night flight had been completed.*

The following day, Whitehall residents boasted that their community was "surrounded by air beacon lights."

Despite progress in other directions, the ninety-mile section between Helena and Great Falls remained unlit and suitable only for daytime flying. In 1935, Great Falls was the only major urban center in the state that did not have 'round-the-clock air service. For unknown reasons, the Bureau of Air Commerce seemed reluctant to install beacons on the route. Subsequently, in January 1937, the chambers of commerce of Helena and Great Falls, along with local civic clubs, launched an intensive campaign to secure federal funding to light the route. Prior to that, in September 1936, they obtained leases from the Montana Department of State Lands (now the

Department of Natural Resources and Conservation) for two beacons, one near Montana native and Hollywood actor Gary Cooper's ranch. It wasn't until late August 1937, however, that work began in earnest to install five beacons between Helena and Great Falls.

During the late 1930s, the Bureau of Air Commerce, usually at the urging of local civic groups, established branch airway routes, or cut-offs, of the longer transcontinental routes. In 1937, the bureau established cut-offs of the Northern Transcontinental Airway Route from the Strawberry Butte Beacon near Logan in the Gallatin valley west through Three Forks, Butte and to Deer Lodge, where it rejoined with the main route. The bureau constructed six beacons at Three Forks, Lewis and Clark Cavern, Cardwell, Silver Bow, Galen and the Deer Lodge Airport. The Homestake Beacon functioned as a hub for two airway routes.

The General Airways Division of the Civil Aeronautics Authority (CAA) established the third and last airway route in Montana in 1939. The Inland Airway Route stretched between Cheyenne, Wyoming, and Great Falls, Montana. The route was flown by Inland Air Lines, based out of Cheyenne. In May 1939, the CAA requested bids for the installation of twelve airway beacons between Billings and Great Falls. Contractors N.E. Bushy and A.L. Porter of Dallas, Texas, got the job and erected the towers on this segment of the route. Work began on the project after the beginning of the then-new federal fiscal year on July 1 and was well underway by the end of August. Ten of the twelve beacons were hooked directly to Montana Power Company transmission lines, while the two towers in the Snowy Mountains relied on self-starting generators. The CAA had installed twenty-seven beacons between Cheyenne and Billings by September 1, 1939; they were operational between Billings and Great Falls by December 1 that year.

The beacon system laid the groundwork for the modern Federal Airway System. Historian Edward P. Warner noted in 1937:

> *Of all American contributions to the technique of air transport operations flying at night by beacons was the greatest. How great it was, and how far it put the United States ahead of the rest of the world, was attested to by the fact that, as late as the early 1930s, when Americans were flying more or less routinely at night, Europeans were still fingering the hem of the idea of night flying.*

The lighted airway beacon system flourished nationwide into the mid-1960s. In 1958, the newly established Federal Aviation Administration (FAA) took jurisdiction over the navigation systems along designated airways. The agency quickly began to assess its resources and questioned the necessity of the national beacon system, given the advances in technology since World War II. Beginning in 1964, the FAA made several attempts to decommission the airway beacons, but opposition in Montana by pilots, the Montana Aeronautics Commission (MAC) and the state's congressional delegation prevented the shutdown. In 1965, the agency, with the assistance of the MAC, again surveyed the beacons under federal control. As a result of the survey, the FAA decommissioned all but eight of its beacons and transferred responsibility of the others to the MAC. The commission maintained eighteen former FAA beacons and relocated thirteen others to local publicly owned airports and museums. By 1971, the MAC operated and maintained fourteen beacons in the mountainous western part of Montana.

By the early twenty-first century, the obsolescence of the system, the cost of maintaining it, a shrinking maintenance budget and lack of qualified staff to maintain the lights all contributed to the Montana Department of Transportation's decision in October 2017 to decommission the beacon system.* Because some controversy surrounded the decision, Mike Tooley, MDT director, formed a panel, the Airway Beacon Working Group (ABWG), to study the issue and make recommendations regarding the future of the airway beacons. To that end, the ABWG solicited public comments and held three public informational meetings in Billings, Missoula and Helena in the summer of 2017. Based on public and written comments and the recommendations of the ABWG, the director decided on October 26, 2017, to decommission all but the Lookout Pass and St. Regis Beacons. By 2020, the MDT had transferred ownership of the remaining fourteen beacons to private individuals, public entities and the Idaho Aviation Heritage Foundation. As of this writing (May 2023), most of the decommissioned beacons still light the night sky, a tribute to their contribution to the history of aviation in Montana and the United States.

---

* In 1972, the Montana Aeronautics Commission became a division within the Montana Department of Commerce. Nineteen years later, in 1991, the state legislature transferred the division to the newly designated Montana Department of Transportation.

ANCIENT LANDSCAPES

THE CRAZY MOUNTAINS

The scenic Crazy Mountains form an "island" mountain range near the center of the Crazy Mountain Basin. Unlike many mountain ranges that are blocks of crust uplifted during faulting, the Crazy Mountains were formed by igneous activity. About fifty million years ago, magma (molten rock) traveled through thick layers of sedimentary rock as it pushed up to the surface. The molten rock cooked (metamorphosed) the surrounding shale to form a hard, resistant rock known as hornfels. Time and erosion stripped the softer sedimentary rock surrounding the intrusion, leaving the resistant core towering over six thousand feet above the adjacent plains.

The Big Timber Stock is the largest intrusion within the Crazy Mountains. It is exposed in the higher southern end of the range, whereas smaller stocks appear to the north. The igneous activity associated with the stocks was also responsible for the emplacement of impressive dike swarms, hundreds of dikes (magma-filled cracks in the older sedimentary rocks) that form a roughly radial pattern around the intrusions. These dikes often form narrow linear ridges that extend up the mountainsides. They persist because they are more resistant to erosion than the surrounding shales and sandstones of the Fort Union Formation.

The Crazy Mountains were the only mountains in central Montana that were tall enough to support glaciers during the last ice age. Glacial action carved the jagged peaks, cirque basins and deep valleys that characterize the present landscape. Today, the Crazy Mountains contain about fifty glaciers, perennial snowfields and numerous alpine lakes. The largest glacier is Grasshopper Glacier near Cottonwood Lake.

An igneous upheaval formed the Crazy Mountains about fifty million years ago. The range's jagged peaks have great spiritual significance to the Crow people. *Hager/MDT.*

Called Awaxaawippiia by the Apsaalooka (Crow) Natives, the Crazy Mountains were places of refuge and protection for the tribe. The Apsaalookas' enemies would not follow them into the mountains. Because of their great spiritual power, Awaxaawippiia continues to be an important vision quest site for the tribe. Famed Chief Plenty Coups had a vision there in 1857; in the vision, he said, the end of the Plains Native way of life was shown to him.

There are several stories about how the mountains got their current name. The most popular story says that a woman who was traveling across the plains with a wagon train went insane. She escaped from the party and was found near these mountains. So, they were called the Crazy Woman Mountains, a name that was eventually shortened. The Crazy Mountains were an important landmark for Bozeman Trail migrants in the Yellowstone valley. This district was great cow and sheep country in the days of the open range, and there are still a number of large ranches in this vicinity, though they are now surrounded by fencing.

16

A TRAIL THROUGH DAYS GONE BY

Black Otter Trail

The 1930s was the first golden age for automobile tourism in Montana. It was during that stormy decade that the state and its counties and cities developed tourism programs that included a variety of plans to draw tourists to the Treasure State and keep them for a while. Tourists brought money to cash-strapped communities in the state during the Great Depression. The Montana Highway Department developed an extensive tourism program that included highway maps, roadside historical markers and the port of entry stations, among other things. Lewis and Clark Cavern and the Little Bighorn Battlefield became important tourist attractions, and both the Beartooth Highway and Going to the Sun Road were opened to traffic. Many places, like Billings, also developed plans to draw tourists in. There was a lot of history to promote in Billings and the surrounding area. Not only was there the Little Bighorn Battlefield, pictograph caves and other points of historical interest, but the city itself was an important nexus of Montana history. The rimrocks provided an excellent vantage point to show off past events in the area and brag about the Magic City. The Billings Commercial Club was poised to take advantage of that fact to make the city a major draw for tourists. The result was the establishment of a scenic road atop the rims: the Black Otter Trail.

Designed by Yellowstone County surveyor Charles E. Durland, the road stretched from Kelly Mountain on the east end of the rims overlooking the fairgrounds west to the *Range Rider of the Yellowstone* statue near the

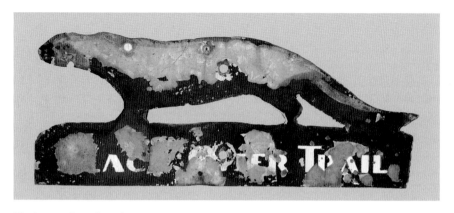

Black otter-shaped markers once guided motorists to areas of special interest on the trail. *Author's collection.*

municipal airport. A loop encircled Skeleton Cliff and provided an excellent vantage point for Billings, the Yellowstone valley and the Midland Empire Fairgrounds. Observers on the loop could see seven mountain ranges in the Billings vicinity. Works Progress Administration (WPA) crews started work on the road in March 1936 and built about 30 percent of the road before a lack of funding forced them to abandon the project—they never returned. Yellowstone County furnished the materials, construction equipment and labor to complete the project. In 1937, the Billings City Council opened the road to traffic.

When completed, the trail included turnouts at scenic and historic points. Guard walls and retaining walls composed of native sandstone kept traffic on the road and prevented motorists from taking the quick way to the base of the rims. Seventeen historical markers along the route echoed the appearance of the Montana Highway Department's roadside markers: they were composed of log support posts, concrete bases faced with stone and wood sign boards. The markers addressed important events and places that could be seen from the trail. This included the site of a Crow Native camp that was decimated by smallpox in 1837 or 1838, the site of the 1823 Immel and Jones massacre, the former townsite of Coulson and the Boot Hill Cemetery, among others. Concrete pyramids veneered in cobblestones held metal pipes with telescopes mounted on them. An ingenious device on Kelly Mountain pointed out the different mountain ranges visible from the trail. In many ways, the new trail was a smaller facsimile of the Going to the Sun Road. Importantly, the trail also incorporated the grave site of Luther S. "Yellowstone" Kelly. Kelly was a renowned scout for the U.S. Army during the Indian Wars. When he died in 1928, he asked to be buried on top of the rimrocks overlooking his beloved Yellowstone valley.

The Tourist Committee of the Billings Commercial Club, the predecessor of the chamber of commerce, took charge of the promotion of the scenic road. In 1938, the committee officially named the route Black Otter's Trail "in honor of an Indian chief who was buried near the grave of Yellowstone Kelly." The committee manufactured a lengthy history of the Crow chief, stating that he died in a battle with another tribe in 1861 and was buried somewhere on top of the rims. Unfortunately, Black Otter appears to have been a fiction developed by the commercial club. There is no evidence, including from Crow tribal elders, that Black Otter ever existed. Regardless, in 1938, the club began to distribute tourist folders with maps of Black Otter Trail on them. The folders touted the historical sites motorists could see and visit. These included Kelly's grave site, the Place of Skulls, the old site of the steamboat port of Coulson and Boot Hill Cemetery.

The National Youth Administration and the local high school's art classes provided signage for the trail. The historical markers were a particular target of vandalism almost from the beginning. They needed replacing on an annual basis. Other promotional schemes developed by the tourist committee included the construction of an observation tower and the erection of a tepee on Kelly Mountain near Yellowstone Kelly's grave. One

During the Great Depression, Billings boosters built Black Otter Trail to draw tourists and day-trippers to the rimrocks overlooking the city. *Author's collection.*

idea of questionable taste was the planned installation of a replica Native burial scaffold next to the trail. A persistent problem was the road itself. Since the road was a gravel-surfaced facility, its promoters annually badgered the county commissioners and others to pave it. There never seemed to be enough money in the county budget to do the work. In fact, it wasn't until the 1960s that the county finally paved Black Otter Trail.

In 1944, the commercial club's tourism committee sponsored a contest to stimulate interest in the trail during World War II. The goal of the contest was "to secure ideas and designs for appropriate landscaping and furnishings" for the postwar period. The winner, famed Billings landscape artist LeRoy Greene, received a war bond for his suggestions about landscaping the road. Newspaper articles in the *Billings Gazette* suggest the trail had become somewhat of a headache for the tourist committee, Yellowstone County and the City of Billings in the postwar years.

Over the years, however, the original intent of Black Otter Trail faded. Chronic vandalism caused the chamber of commerce to remove the telescopes and historical markers in the 1960s. Littered by empty beer cans and trash, the trail was the site of parties, murders and other nefarious activities. The city and county generally neglected the road. Since the 1990s, however, Black Otter Trail has experienced a renaissance. The road has been incorporated into the Swords Park Trail, and the Yellowstone Kelly grave site was refurbished in 2017. The trail was listed in the National Register of Historic Places in 2007. Black Otter Trail once again provides motorists and pedestrians spectacular views of the Yellowstone valley and passes through an area steeped in Montana history.

MONTANA ROADSIDES

STONEY THE BULL

At one time, investors had big plans for Clearwater Junction in Missoula County. In 1966, three Missoula business partners, including Bud Lake, formed a company to develop two hundred acres at Clearwater Junction into a resort. After engineering a land swap with the old Montana Fish and Game Commission, the men obtained a beer and liquor license. They opened the Clearwater Bar and Lounge in 1967. By the following year, the newly christened Clearwater Resort included a service station, gift shop and snack bar; a restaurant soon followed. Bud Lake managed the operation at the junction of Montana Highways 200 and 83. The resort mostly catered to local residents but also drew visitors from around the country and Canada. The bar featured live country music on the weekends, and the restaurant provided smorgasbord meals every day.

In late 1970, the ownership of the resort passed to Montana natives Mark Curtiss and Warren Stone. They planned to add a modern campground featuring rental tepees, A-frame guest houses, a playground, restrooms, laundromat and motel. Unfortunately, their big plans for the Clearwater Resort never panned out. The business has operated under different owners and several names over the years. It even survived two devastating fires. The site continues to function as an important stop for travelers and area residents at Clearwater Junction.

The big bull at the junction is a genuine Montana landmark. In 1970 or 1971, Clearwater Resort manager Warren Stone purchased the twenty-by-twelve-foot fiberglass Hereford bull from an agent of the Sculptured Advertising Company for $5,000. Based in Sparta,

Located at the junction of Montana Highways 83 and 200, *Stoney the Bull* provides a memorable point of reference for residents and tourists. *Rob Park/MDT.*

Wisconsin, the company specialized in the manufacture of larger-than-life animals for businesses and roadside attractions. All the sculptures came with trailers that many animals, like *Stoney the Bull*, still stand on. Over the years, Stoney became a popular roadside attraction at Clearwater Junction. "Turn at the big cow" is a catchphrase used by many when providing directions to area destinations. *Stoney* received its first makeover in 1998, when a Butte auto body shop patched over two hundred bullet holes in it, repainted it and fabricated a new fiberglass tail to replace the original tail, which had been stolen. Most recently, in 2021, a Missoula body shop reattached a horn, patched another thirty-two bullet holes, fixed the tail and gave it a fresh coat of paint. *Stoney* still stands watch at the junction, a welcome and popular sight for travelers on the highway year-round.

17

FOR A GOOD SNACK OR A TASTY MEAL

Matt's Place

Drive-in restaurants have been a fixture on the urban landscape for well over a century. Drive-ins flourished as part of the mobility afforded to motorists after World War I and the explosion in the number of automobiles on the nation's highways. Montana was no stranger to drive-ins, as the first appeared in the state in the 1930s. The first modern drive-in restaurant in the United States opened in Dallas, Texas, in 1921. The Pig Stand was the first restaurant built specifically to serve meals to motorists in their cars. The roadside eatery was the brainchild of Dallas physician R.W. Jackson and entrepreneur J.G. Kirby, who is rumored to have groused that "people with cars are so lazy that they don't want to get out of them to eat." An immediate success, the number of Pig Stands mushroomed throughout Texas.

Although the drive-in was a Texas innovation, it was in California that they reached their ultimate form and became most associated with the free-wheeling lifestyle of that state's citizens. For many Americans on the go, drive-ins ideally suited their lifestyles. Consequently, the number of drive-ins boomed nationwide, becoming a firmly entrenched part of popular culture. By 1927, drive-ins based on the California models had spread throughout the United States, catering to both regional and national tastes in food. In Montana, the national fad of serve-in-your-car restaurants is more difficult to track, as they were not listed by type in the city directories with illustrated advertising until the early 1950s. But what may be the first drive-in in the state still stands near the intersection of North Montana Street and Rowe Road in Butte: Matt's Place.

When Matt's Place opened in Butte in 1930, it was one of seventy-eight restaurants in that city. All but two were located uptown; Matt's and the Interstate Company were located on South Montana Street. Throughout the 1930s and 1940s, the number of restaurants in Butte averaged around seventy-two. In 1949, only four could be positively identified as drive-in restaurants: Matt's, the Interstate Company, Duck Inn Hamburger Shop and Bill's Drive-In. By 1956, the number of drive-in restaurants in Butte had doubled to eight. Most, however, were located on South Harrison Avenue at the east entrance to the city. The increase in the number of drive-ins in Butte corresponded with a similar increase in Montana's other major cities between 1952 and 1962. Billings led the list with fourteen drive-ins, followed by Great Falls, Butte and Helena.

John and Jennie Korn immigrated to Butte from Austria in 1893 and ran a saloon at 1831 South Montana Street along what was then known as "the Boulevard." They enjoyed the benefits of operating in the city, although their business, located on the west side of South Montana and technically outside the city limits, left them exempt from city taxes. The Korns' saloon operated from about 1911 until Prohibition. John Korn's establishment was equipped with a pavilion out back for dancing and boxing matches, both popular activities in Butte. The family lived and worked in the same South Montana neighborhood where other Austrian immigrants had also settled.

The Korns had two sons, Matt and John Jr. Both young men eventually followed in their father's entrepreneurial footsteps. John established Korn's Shoetorium, a longtime fixture in uptown Butte. Matt was more of a risk-taker. In 1930, as the nation gloomily looked toward a depressed economy, he had a novel idea based on something he had seen in his travels to California.

In June 1930, Matt Korn purchased an old placer mining claim from the City of Butte. The property was located near his old neighborhood on the east side of South Montana Street, just inside the city limits. It was less than two blocks from his father's old saloon and a few blocks away from the family home at 1803 South Washington Street. The property had been incorporated into the city as the Montana Avenue Addition in September 1890. Matt either took over a shack that stood on the property or obtained an outbuilding from a residential site owned by the State Highway Commission.

Matt Korn opened a sandwich shop in the building and named it Matt's Place. Later, Korn owned and operated a tavern, the Shack, across Rowe Road to the east. Like the new places he had seen in California, the eatery had a drive-up window so that customers could order from their cars. The little shack had no inside or curb service at first, only window service. By 1931, the small one-story restaurant was in its present location, perhaps moved a short distance to the edge of Rowe Road. This street, although roughed out along the northeast corner of Matt's property, had scarcely been planned and was still undefined. A tourist park located across Placer Street still stands as a reminder of those early days when motorcars made family travel an adventure.

Matt's Place was typical of drive-in restaurants in the United States in the late 1920s and early 1930s. Instead of the flashy, modernistic and brightly lit drive-ins of the 1950s, Matt's Place was simple and unadorned. Matt Korn imported the idea for the business from southern California, then the site of the most drive-in restaurants in the country. The nature of the business required that it be centralized while making maximum use of the roadside frontage for parking. Matt's was ideally located near the intersection of South Montana Street, a major north–south thoroughfare in Butte, and U.S. Highway 10–South, Montana's primary east–west interstate highway. Unlike drive-ins in California, however, Matt's did not rely on extensive signage, neon lights or singular architecture to draw customers. Matt did

Along with its great food, Matt's Place was famous in Butte for its friendly staff. *Butte–Silver Bow County Archives.*

occasionally advertise the business in local newspapers. But Matt's Place relied primarily on its "sparkling cleanliness, speed and good food" for its success. The existing menu boards show meals that were quick to prepare and serve. Like its counterparts in the east, Matt's also served regional favorites, such as barbecue beef and hamburger with a fried egg.

Matt's Place quickly became a local hangout for a population with few recreational opportunities. Among the neighborhood customers was Mabel Waddell. Mabel was born in Chicago before her parents came to Butte, where her father was in the wholesale grocery business and her mother worked for the Manhattan Bakery. Her parents separated, and times were tough in the 1930s. Mabel and a friend frequently walked from Iowa Street to the cemeteries along South Montana. When her friend's mother gave them a nickel, they would stop at Matt's Place for a special treat. "Grape Juice Matt" was famous for his concoction he adapted from his father's wine recipe.

Matt Korn married Betty Kabalin in 1931. Reportedly, the wedding took place in a plane as it flew over Butte. (Matt had a pilot's license.) The couple spent their wedding night serving customers who packed the small parking lot until the restaurant closed at 1:00 a.m. Business was never slow, and by 1934, the Korns had added upstairs living quarters to the restaurant. Korn had also added a horseshoe counter with indoor seating for eight by 1936.

In 1936, when Mabel Waddell was in high school, she began working for Matt after school. Mabel changed her name because Matt Korn had "Mae" embroidered on her uniform. She joined the staff as one of seven carhops. They worked nonstop six days a week until closing.

Matt Korn made very good profits, but he was difficult to work for and paid his help low wages. He didn't believe in Christmas gifts or bonuses, and the carhops held their Christmas gift exchange in secret, drawing names out of each other's pockets on the sly. Matt also did not believe in gimmicks and always said that if you see someone giving something away, it's a sure sign he is in trouble. "Never skimp on quality or quantity" was Matt Korn's dictum. He was a product of the Depression. Mae's last paycheck in 1943, for a six-day week working eight hours a day, was $17.50.

In 1943, Mae Waddell was still working at night for Matt Korn, was engaged to marry teamster Louis Laurence and was about to graduate from beauty school. She had saved enough money to buy a beauty shop in Boulder, but when the deal fell through, Matt persuaded the couple to buy the restaurant from him. On March 1, 1943, Matt's Place reopened under new ownership. Like Matt and his wife, Louis and Mae spent their

Established by Matt Korn in 1930, Matt's Place was the first drive-in restaurant in Montana. It was famous for its excellent food. *Rob Park/MDT.*

honeymoon waiting on customers. They couldn't afford a new sign, so the name Matt's Place remained. Although it was wartime, customers were never lacking. Louis and Mae had to watch their rations and go all over Butte to get the groceries Matt's Place required.

It was always hard work, but Mae and Louis employed family members, including Mae's mother and sisters, and the place was always busy. The 1940s, before the advent of television, were the best years. People spent their evenings at the theater or the movies and ended up at Matt's Place afterward. High school kids came to Matt's Place after school, games and prom dressed in their elegant finery.

In 1950, the Laurences made the last changes to their business. They added the Coke machine, a Proctor Silex coffee pot, knotty pine interior paneling and two hand-painted photomurals of the Rockies. All remain today. They also enclosed an upstairs porch so their daughter could have a safe place to play. Except for Matt's long-gone grape juice, the menu, including the original nutburger (a burger with a "protein blast of peanuts"), remained as it had since the 1930s. The most significant change the restaurant experienced was the construction of Interstate 90 in 1964. Matt's Place was such a popular Butte establishment, patronized by a regular clientele, that the interstate was no hindrance to business.

Louis Laurence passed away in 1962. Mae considered her options and then took over Matt's Place herself. Through the decades, more than twenty-eight family members worked for her at various times. Matt's Place was written up in *Gourmet* magazine and *Montana Magazine* several times and was featured in the *Chicago Tribune* and *Horizon Air* magazine. In 1998, the Butte Chamber of Commerce named Mae Laurence the Small Business Person of the Year, an honor of which she was most proud. In 2016, the restaurant won a coveted James Beard Foundation Award. Mae Laurence ran the drive-in until her death at the age of one hundred in January 2013. Four months before her passing, she was the grand marshal of Butte's annual Fourth of July parade. As a side note, this writer had the best hamburger, French fries and milkshake of his life there in the early 2000s with Mae holding center court inside the horseshoe-shaped counter.

Matt's Place is a classic example of the revolutionary drive-in restaurants that swept the nation in the late 1920s and 1930s. But unlike the restaurant chains that now line Harrison Avenue, Matt's Place had no playground, no splashy advertising and no precooked menu items. Over the years, other restaurants have operated nearby, but Matt's Place has outlasted them all by decades. It is one of Montana's first drive-ins, representing the mom-and-pop operations that once flourished across the nation but that rarely survived the fast-food chain invasion of later decades. Matt's Place evolved to its present appearance during its first five years and has changed little since 1950. It has been a Butte landmark since that time, and its nostalgic ambiance is still indicative of that era.

ANCIENT LANDSCAPES

THE GREAT INLAND SEAWAY AND EAGLE SANDSTONE

About eighty million years ago, the Billings area was near the shore of a great inland ocean called the Western Interior Seaway that stretched from the present-day Gulf Coast to the Arctic Ocean. Rivers that drained the highlands to the west carried sediment into the seaway, and near-shore currents concentrated the sand, creating barrier islands. As the sea level alternately rose and fell, the barrier islands migrated, forming an extensive layer of chiefly fine-grained sand across much of central Montana. The sand was eventually buried, compacted and cemented into the rocks we now see as the rimrocks in the Yellowstone valley. Geologists have named it eagle sandstone. When observed from the south, the rimrocks reveal low-angle, westward-dipping cross beds called accretion surfaces. These surfaces record the deposition of sand that was washed over the barrier and deposited on the other side by waves, causing the bar to accrete or grow shoreward.

The seaway was shallow, warm and probably no more than a few hundred feet deep. Yet it was home to a wide variety of aquatic life. Oysters lived in dense banks along the shore, while tentacled ammonites fed on clams that lived in the shallow water offshore; sharks also cruised the shallows, preying on whatever animals appeared tasty to them. For several million years, two predators were at the top of the food chain in the sea: the long-necked plesiosaurs and the snakelike mosasaurs. Neither were dinosaurs but were air-breathing reptiles that had adapted to living in the oceans.

The Yellowstone valley's rimrocks formed as sandy beach deposits about eighty million years ago, when dinosaurs still roamed the area. *Kristi Hager/MDT.*

The rimrocks near the confluence of the Yellowstone River and Alkali Creek in Billing Heights is one of Montana's historic hot spots. Natives utilized the area for at least eight thousand years before William Clark passed through the area in July 1806. Although it is known as Crow Country, the Blackfeet, Lakota and Northern Cheyenne were also frequent visitors to the area. Near here on May 31, 1823, Blackfeet warriors ambushed and killed seven Missouri Fur Company trappers under the command of Michael Immel and Robert Jones. The eagle sandstone of the rims provided a spectacular backdrop for the rip-roaring settlement of Coulson in the 1870s and for Billings from the early 1880s, just after the arrival of the Northern Pacific Railway.

18

DIGGING INTO THE PAST

The Highway Commission and Pictograph Caves

In June 1937, amateur archaeologists discovered a wealth of cultural materials in the wake of a rainstorm in two caves on Empty Gulch a few miles southeast of Billings. Within a short time, because of intense lobbying by archaeologists, civic groups, college officials and others, the Works Progress Administration (WPA) funded an extensive archaeological excavation in pictograph and ghost caves. The digs revealed that the caves had been occupied by Montana's Natives for at least 4,500 years. Importantly, the caves also displayed a gallery of wall paintings, called pictographs, that dated to around 500 CE. The site represented a significant find that would become the basis of our understanding of man's presence on the northern Great Plains. It would also generate debate over the artifacts taken from the site and how the caves should be preserved and interpreted by the public. Pictograph Cave is a world-class heritage site that became a major draw for visitors from all over the world. From 1938 to 1941, the Montana State Highway Commission (SHC) not only purchased the site but also partially funded the excavation of the caves and built a museum there. The highway commission's efforts made the site a significant tourist draw and led to its eventual designation as a National Historic Landmark.

During the Great Depression, the SHC played a vital role in the development of the state's tourism program. Along with implementing roadside historical markers, highway maps, roadside picnic areas and port of entry stations, it promoted tourist attractions, like the Little Bighorn Battlefield. It was all intended to draw people to Montana and keep them here to invest their money in the state's economy during the dark days of the Depression. The highway commission purchased the Pictograph Caves site in 1938, specifically to exploit its tourism potential. The discovery of important archaeological remains at Pictograph Caves fit nicely into the department's program to promote Montana's natural, scenic and cultural resources.

The WPA and H. Melville Sayre of the Montana School of Mines in Butte began the large-scale excavation of Pictograph Caves in 1937. At that time, there was some concern about the ownership of the caves and their continued availability to archaeologists. Sayre met often with the highway commission's plans engineer Robert H. "Bob" Fletcher. Fletcher was the brain behind the implementation of the SHC's tourism programs. Fletcher, who knew Sayre through their association with the Montana Society of Natural History, was already aware of the Pictograph Caves. The men met in late August or early September 1937. When Sayre hinted to Fletcher that the property could be purchased for a reasonable price "by some department of the state," he was quick to offer Sayre his help. He agreed to pass the information on to state highway engineer Don McKinnon, the highway department's liaison with the highway commissioners. Both Fletcher and McKinnon believed that the site's proximity to newly completed U.S. Highway 87 might deflect criticism from what Fletcher termed a "not-too-prehistoric-site-minded public." The commission consisted of three government-appointed individuals. Two commissioners, McKinnon and Fletcher believed, might be inclined to consider Sayre's proposal.

Great Falls banker and real estate broker Lee M. Ford was the son of Robert Simpson Ford, one of the founders of the Montana cattle industry in the 1870s. Ford was a member of the Great Falls Chamber of Commerce's Good Roads Committee and served as vice-president of the Montana Historical Society. Importantly for Fletcher and Sayre's plans, Ford was an avid collector of Native artifacts. Billings businessman and booster John M. Wheeler also sat on the SHC and would play a critical role in the caves' future. A tireless promoter of Billings and the surrounding area, Wheeler was well-informed of the Montana School of Mines's (MSM) activities at Pictograph Caves through his association with the Billings Commercial Club. Missoula real estate manager Lloyd Hague was the third member of the commission.

On September 20, 1937, commission secretary William Whipps presented Sayre's proposal to the highway commission for the purchase of the Pictograph Caves site. In his letter to the SHC, Sayre proposed to "make this spot a roadside campsite and beautification and education project." Sayre

INDIAN CAVES, NEAR BILLINGS, MONTANA

Pictograph Caves is a National Historic Landmark site. It has yielded evidence of human occupation dating back at least 1,500 years. *Author's collection*.

wrote that an option had already been acquired on the forty-acre property from its owner, Nora Morehouse, with a purchase price of $400. The WPA was currently leasing the property, but the lease was to expire in June 1938. Although Sayre stressed that there was no hurry to secure a purchase option, he pressed the commission for an answer. The commission considered Sayre's proposal and pronounced it a "very meritorious undertaking." Although the SHC was not sure it could purchase the property with federal funds, it elected to obtain the forty-acre tract from Morehouse for the agreed-on price under certain conditions.

The commissioners stipulated that a building be constructed on site to function as a museum to "display and exhibit the artifacts which are being excavated and the said artifacts shall be kept there and not removed to some other place." While the commission was adamant that it was not responsible for the construction of the building, it did offer to loan the project sponsors furnishings and equipment to construct a museum on the site. The panel also specified that the City of Billings and/or Yellowstone County furnish tour guides and custodians for the site during the tourist season.

In November 1937, former highway commissioner Grover Cisel and Billings postmaster and civic promoter Mearl Fagg reported to the highway commission that arrangements had been completed to construct the museum as a county WPA project. The commissioners agreed to provide architectural plans for the museum based on the roadside museums currently under development at the highway department. The museum was to include dioramas, photographs, maps, charts and typical artifacts excavated from the site. The commissioners authorized its right-of-way agents to purchase as much of the property as possible with the allotted $400 for the project. The highway commission utilized state funds to buy the property, thus bypassing the federal constraints. In January 1938, the SHC purchased a little over twenty-two acres, including the caves, from Nora Morehouse for "use as a public roadside camp and as the site for a possible museum to house the excavated artifacts for public exhibition."

Concurrently with the commission's purchase of the Pictograph Caves site, the Billings Commercial Club formed the Indian Caves Development Committee (ICDC) to work with the WPA, the highway commission and the Montana School of Mines to continue the excavation and promotion of the caves. At the committee's first meeting, held in January 1938, its members discussed the plans for the proposed museum, which would cost Yellowstone County $525 to construct with WPA labor. The ICDC and Yellowstone County Commissioners then submitted an application to the WPA for the construction of the museum. Billings WPA representative Frank Bowman promised to prepare the necessary estimates for the carpentry work and foundation construction.

The SHC eagerly assumed its new role as owner of the scientifically important and locally popular archaeological site. The commission, at least initially, didn't provide monetary support for the operation. Instead, it supplied men and equipment to survey the site and build some small construction projects. Walter Vanaman, a highway department surveyor, worked with the WPA and ICDC and often assisted with the excavations. He occasionally acted as a tour guide for visitors to the site. For all of Fletcher's interest in the site and his critical role as the highway commission's acquisition of the property, there is no evidence he ever visited the caves during the WPA years.

From 1937 until 1942, when the WPA's involvement in the project ceased, the highway commission concentrated its attention on the artifacts recovered from the site. The educational value of the artifacts was less important to the highway commission than their location, who was in possession of them and how they could be best used. The commission's concern was genuine, since the artifacts technically belonged to it.

The SHC stipulated that H. Melville Sayre continue to supervise the excavation and make periodic progress reports to the commission. It also ordered that a duplicate set of artifacts be deposited with the WPA for final disposition at the Smithsonian Institute. In June 1938, Sayre sent Fletcher a letter outlining his plans for placing interpretive signs around the Pictograph Caves site. Like Fletcher's highway historical markers, these signs were chatty but contained considerable information about the excavation, the artifacts and the people who once lived there. In addition to the interpretive markers, Sayre proposed placing up to forty trail signs at the site. Unfortunately, there is no record of Fletcher's response to Sayre's plans, and it is unclear if the markers were ever installed.

While Sayre and amateur archaeologist Oscar Lewis were concerned about the scientific importance of the archaeological site, the members of the ICDC were more interested in how the site could be used to the benefit of the Billings economy. The committee's meetings always concentrated on the economic potential of the caves to the city and county. At its June 1938 meeting, the ICDC hired "four boys" to act as guides at the caves for the increasing number of tourists who were visiting the site. Its members also proposed sponsoring a pageant at the caves with Crow and Blackfeet Natives and perhaps conducting a community "sing" there one evening a week during the summer. The committee provided cases for the exhibits in the Commercial Club lobby and arranged for a similar exhibit at the newly opened highway department museum in Laurel. By August 1938, Fletcher had informed the committee that it needed to complete a plan for the design, installation and arrangement of the exhibit cases at the museum located at the caves site. The highway commission had the final authority over what exhibits the ICDC placed in the museum.

Beginning in 1938, Sayre agitated for a laboratory facility to process and catalog the artifacts removed from the caves. In late November, he established the laboratory in the basement of the Lewistown Civic Center. He did not, however, have the permission of the project's sponsors to do this. In fact, the highway commissioners had specifically stated when they agreed to purchase the site that the artifacts were not to be removed from the immediate vicinity of the caves.

In December 1938, the WPA informed the Indian Caves Committee that the School of Mines would discontinue its sponsorship of the Pictograph Caves project the following month. The committee heard the first rumblings of the problem that would occupy the attention of the highway commission for the next two years. The committee felt that it could not design the appropriate exhibit cases until it knew what artifacts would be available for display at the museum. Further, the committee asked highway commissioner and regular committee attendee John Wheeler to "secure the material excavated from the cave in storage at Lewistown and other cases not known to members of the Committee and that these items should be brought to Billings and stored at the Eastern Montana Normal School."* The school's president Dr. L.B. McMullen also agreed to consult with the highway commission about possibly sponsoring the excavation slated for the 1939 season once the artifacts had been returned to Billings from Lewistown.

The artifacts issue increasingly dominated discussions about the project in succeeding SHC meetings. In early January 1939, Lee Ford reported that the "artifacts which had been removed [from] Ghost Caves…had not been delivered for placing and exhibition in the museum…and that necessary action should be taken to insure this being done." Commission members Wheeler and Lloyd Hague authorized fellow commissioner Ford to conduct a field investigation into the problem and allowed him the use of highway funds to make arrangements for the shipment of the artifacts to the museum at the cave site. Ford's attempts to pry the artifacts away from the Lewistown Chamber of Commerce proved unsuccessful, and they remained in storage at the city's civic center until late 1940.

Sayre's unauthorized removal of the artifacts to the Lewistown laboratory took up considerable time at the May 1939 highway commission meeting. Ford's failure to obtain the artifacts caused dismay among the commission members because they felt they were the rightful owners.

A review of the records and minute entries conclusively indicates that this action was taken in contravention and violation of the agreement entered into, and the Commission decided to take steps looking to the return of the artifacts to the museum at Billings.…That the artifacts were removed from real property belonging to the [SHC], *that they are considered the property of this department and that unless they are returned willingly legal steps will be taken to enforce their return.*

By November, the issue had not been resolved, and the artifacts continued to languish in Lewistown.

In mid-November, Fletcher reported to his bosses that he, along with the ICDC and college president McMullen, had not yet selected any artifacts for display purposes at either the local museum or in the highway department building in Helena. Perhaps hoping that Fletcher's more easygoing manner would produce results, the commissioners authorized him to act on their

* Now Montana State University–Billings.

behalf "in collecting and assembling a display of artifacts for the museum at the [site] and for this department." Further, the commissioners specified that he make the necessary trips to Lewistown and "report the actions taken in his findings from time to time."

Fletcher later placed the blame for the artifact controversy squarely on Melville Sayre. He attributed the problem to Sayre's drinking and personality problems. It is doubtful Fletcher was aware of Sayre's connection to Lewistown through his second wife, since he claimed that the artifacts were moved to the city without "rhyme or reason." In any case, the engineer had a difficult time convincing the Lewistown Chamber of Commerce that the artifacts were the property of the state highway commission and should be released to him. Sayre had apparently promised the chamber of commerce that the artifacts would be displayed there and consequently remain in the city for an indefinite period.

By late December, Fletcher still had not obtained the artifacts from Lewistown. He met with the WPA Division of Professional and Service Projects director Annabell Edinger in Butte about possible solutions to the problem. While Eastern Montana Normal School had largely sponsored the excavation project in 1939, Edinger suggested the SHC take over sponsorship of the project to cement its claim to the artifacts. Edinger also proposed that the highway commission establish other roadside museums in Montana to display the artifacts taken from Pictograph Caves.

The highway commissioners were interested in possibly sponsoring the 1940 Pictograph Caves excavation project. On January 25, 1940, Edinger and other WPA officials met with the SHC to discuss the proposal. Again, the WPA suggested that the commission construct roadside museums in Montana adjacent to primary and state highways. The commissioners again denied the request because of the "main difficulty with projects of this character is to obtain the providing of maintenance and caretakers locally." The commission ordered Fletcher, however, to contact communities to develop some museum projects. From the available records, the highway commission's instructions to Fletcher were largely superficial, and he made no real effort to identify any additional museum sites.

The meeting with the WPA representatives also included discussion about the disposition of the artifacts, which had, by that time, finally been moved to the Eastern Montana Normal School. The WPA initiated a project, under new project director William Mulloy, to sort and classify the material removed from the caves. The highway commission and WPA agreed to form a committee to select artifacts for display at the highway department

Archaeological excavations at Pictograph Cave were ongoing during the 1930s, even while tourists wandered about the dig and peppered the archaeologists with questions. *Timothy Urbaniak Collection.*

building in Helena, the Smithsonian, the Pictograph Caves Museum and "elsewhere as may be decided." Along with Bob Fletcher, the project included representatives from the WPA and Billings Commercial Club (to be selected by commission member Wheeler). Importantly, the SHC stated that once Mulloy had completed his project, the commission would then consider sponsoring additional archaeological projects.

At the December 1940 SHC meeting, Secretary William Whipps read a letter from L.B. McMullen requesting permission from the commission to continue excavations at the caves in 1941. The commissioners replied that they were

> *favorably disposed toward granting the request to continue the excavations but as a condition precedent thereto…insist*[ed] *that a complete set of specimens as excavated be set aside and turned over to the Montana Highway Department. Further, that in view of this condition before formal*

permission is granted to continue excavation, we wish to have executed a formal agreement providing that a complete set of specimens…be turned over to the [department].

Apparently, McMullen was not very clear when telling the commission about who the other sponsors of the project were. The commission, afraid that it may lose control of the artifacts once again, refused to sign any agreement with the WPA until the sponsorship question was clarified.

Nearly a month later, in January 1941, McMullen provided a second letter to the SHC requesting sponsorship for the project. Again, the SHC wanted to know who the other sponsors were. It also wanted an agreement stating that the artifacts would be turned over to the commission before it would allow further excavations at Pictograph Caves. In February 1941, the Pictograph Caves project lost one of its champions at the SHC when Bob Fletcher resigned to take a job as publicity director for the Montana Power Company.

After the United States entered World War II in December 1941, the demands of the war effort forced the SHC's attention away from Pictograph Caves and the disposition of the artifacts. There are no further references to the Pictograph Caves in the Montana Highway Commission meeting minutes. At the request of the State Park Commission, the SHC turned over ownership of the site in January 1949.

The Montana Highway Commission, in its first foray into cultural resource management between 1937 and 1949, was primarily a voluntary administrator concerned about the tourism potential of the site. The SHC's promotion of the site as a tourist attraction, however, was minimal. There was only one mention of the site in the promotional literature distributed in the late 1930s and early 1940s. The 1938 highway commission publication, *Picture Writing*, only mentions Pictograph Caves in passing. Eventually, the site's educational potential was downplayed by the highway commission, and instead, it concentrated on the disposition of the artifacts. Part of this came from the interest of Bob Fletcher and Lee Ford. Fletcher wrote to Montana Historical Society director K. Ross Toole in 1956, "Lee Ford and I would like to have had a representative collection of artifacts from the place. Neither of us got anything."

Today, Pictograph Caves is a state park managed by the Montana Department of Fish, Wildlife and Parks. It once again has a visitors' center, trails and interpretive markers describing the significance of the site to Montana's Natives and to the science of archaeology.

MONTANA ROADSIDES

HEPBURN'S MUSEUM AND THE YELLOWSTONE TRAIL

Despite the crippling effects of the Great Depression, the tourist industry flourished in Montana in the 1930s. Although many Americans were either unemployed or earning minimal wages, many others were still able to take annual vacations and visit local attractions and the state's national parks. To that end, the Montana State Highway Commission formed a unit to advertise the state through promotional literature, colorful highway maps, a network of roadside interpretive markers, museums and informative ports of entry stations on the major highway leading into the Treasure State.

Additional federal funding also allowed the state to significantly improve its highways, thereby improving access to sites that might be visited by out-of-state tourists. Roads that led to the national parks were particularly targeted by local entrepreneurs as worthy of exploitation as they sought to supplement their incomes by creating attractions that tourists might find tempting. U.S. Highway 89 (now Secondary 540) between Livingston and the north entrance to Yellowstone National Park at Gardiner was a potential gold mine for cash-strapped residents living along the highway. The John Hepburn Place is associated with the Great Depression.

A longtime rancher and rockhound in the Paradise valley who had recently retired, John Hepburn realized the opportunity presented by Highway 89. To that end, he built a log museum next to the highway and charged admission for those who wanted to see his amazing collection of geological specimens, fossils and local historical relics. Hepburn's museum included a wide variety of artifacts,

including Miocene fossils acquired from the nearby Hepburn Mesa Formation, geological samples taken from Yellowstone Park and its vicinity, Native items, historical photographs and locally significant historical objects. The museum was a landmark on the highway until the mid-1950s, when the highway department relocated the road to the west side of the Yellowstone River.

At the time Hepburn built his museum, it was located in a remote site in the Paradise valley, far from connections to electrical power lines. Consequently, he and his son, Ralph, installed a wind-powered twenty-four-volt Jacobs generator system to provide electricity to the museum and its outbuildings. The wind-powered electrical system was developed by Jacob and Marcellus Jacobs in the 1920s and quickly became the standard in the industry for rural electricity generation. The Jacobs boys developed the system to provide electricity to their isolated eastern Montana ranch. The original wiring, circuit boards, circuit breakers and gauges are still intact and functional at the old museum site. The Hepburns also harnessed the valley's perpetual wind to power a homemade rock polisher. The rocks polished by the

Opposite: Local rancher, former Yellowstone Park employee and rockhound John Hepburn opened a museum in his home on the main highway between the park and Livingston. *Rob Park/MDT.*

This page: "Mom-and-pop" museums, like Hepburn's, were once important parts of Montana's roadside landscape. Their exhibits were mixes of geological specimens and local historical artifacts. *Rob Park/MDT.*

contraption were sold to museum visitors and tourists who stopped at the site. The rustic appearance of the museum compelled the curious to stop, pay for and examine what was truly a unique collection in Montana.

During the late 1940s and 1950s, Hepburn's museum continued to function as an important roadside attraction on the road between Chico Hot Springs and the north entrance of Yellowstone National Park at Gardiner. The boom in car culture after the war only made the museum more profitable as tourism skyrocketed. Throughout the postwar period, the elderly John Hepburn continued to scour the surrounding area for interesting minerals, fossils and Native and historic artifacts for display in his museum. The museum also functioned as field trip destination for local schools. The museum closed in 1959 after the death of John Hepburn. His collection was dispersed to his surviving family members, with many artifacts being absorbed into other local museum collections.

19

A GIFT FROM THE FEDERAL GOVERNMENT

The Orange Street Tunnel

Formerly known as the Orange Street Underpass, the Orange Street Tunnel is a Missoula landmark. Located on Orange Street just south of the I-90 interchange, it provided access to Missoula's commercial district for the "northsiders" in the neighborhoods north of the Northern Pacific Railway tracks. When completed, the structure changed traffic patterns in Missoula and provided easier and safer access between the north and south sides of the city. It was one of many railroad underpasses built in Montana during the Great Depression. It looks much like it did when it was completed in 1939. In 2020, the Montana Department of Transportation redesignated the underpass as a tunnel because of its length. It is one of two tunnels owned by the MDT, the other being an abandoned Milwaukee Road tunnel about two miles west of Alberton.

Public agitation for the construction of an underpass under the Northern Pacific Railway tracks to connect the north and south sides of Missoula began as early as 1912. Northside residents, including Elizabeth Crawshaw, initiated the campaign for the structure for safety and traffic purposes. Mrs. Crawshaw had lived on North Second Street West, about two blocks north of the future site of the tunnel, since 1901. The Northern Pacific Railway Company (NPRR) supported the construction of an underpass and appropriated money for its construction before the United States' entry into World War I in April 1917 temporarily halted the project.

The public need for a crossing under the NPRR tracks worsened in the 1920s as the number of automobiles on Missoula's streets increased.

On December 12, 1928, the Missoula City Council passed a resolution that authorized Mayor William Beacom to negotiate with the Northern Pacific to identify potential sites for the eventual construction of an underpass. Councilman and future state highway commissioner Lloyd Hague introduced the resolution after he received a petition signed by 525 northsiders. The petition stated that it was "an absolute necessity for the safety of the residents of that section as well as their welfare, that an underpass be constructed under the railroad tracks" at a site yet to be determined. Six days later, on December 18, the city council wrote a letter to NPRR president Charles Donnelly asking for his cooperation to "secure for Missoula the construction of a viaduct under the Northern Pacific tracks." Donnelly responded a week later, promising he would give the council's request his "utmost consideration."

In January 1929, NPRR superintendent J.H. Johnson announced that the railroad would make a study of the Woody Street crossing, the busiest in Missoula. He made no promises that anything would come of the study. The matter languished for eight months before the NPRR revealed that an underpass would cost somewhere between $233,000 and $422,000. Half the cost of the structure would have to be borne by the citizens of Missoula. The stock market crash in 1929 and the onset of the Great Depression again temporarily halted any plans for the underpass.

Hope for the underpass was revived with President Franklin Delano Roosevelt's New Deal in 1933. The *Missoulian* ruminated that the construction of an underpass would provide around five thousand men employment, for which the Federal Recovery Act would supply all the funding. The newspaper speculated that the underpass would be located at either the Woody Street or Stevens Street crossings. Although the NPRR placed guards at the crossings, it was still a hazard because children would dash across the tracks on their way to and from school. Motorists suffered through extended waits for long trains, and emergency vehicles could not get across the tracks when they were occupied by trains. The lack of an underpass created a barrier between the north and south sides of the community.

The elimination of busy at-grade railroad crossings throughout the United States was a hot topic among federal, state and local officials starting around 1912. Prior to 1935, the construction of grade separation structures had been financed by a combination of local and federal funds funneled through the state highway departments. Since 1920, all the states, counties and municipalities in the United States had undertaken grade separation projects. But it wasn't until the Emergency Relief Appropriation Act of 1935 set aside money specifically for that kind of project that there was a substantial number of these projects undertaken by the states, funded 100 percent by the federal government. In Montana, the State Highway Commission obtained the rules and regulations for carrying out the provisions of the act in July 1935. Montana's share of the grade elimination program was $2.7 million. The highway commission awarded the first underpass project in November 1935. Over the next three years, until the commission let the Orange Street Tunnel project, the highway commission funded the construction of thirteen underpasses and twenty-six overhead crossing structures as part of the United States Works Program Grade Crossing Program.

The availability of federal funds for the construction of an underpass in Missoula revived public support for the structure. Concurrent with the circulation of new petitions for the underpass by Missoulians, Mayor Dwight Mason and Councilmen Harry M. Smith and Roy Hamilton declared themselves in support of the project. The *Missoulian* reported, "Money has been allocated for eliminating dangerous railway crossings and Missoulians are starting a campaign for the underpass declare that a proposed underpass here would be one of the most meritorious in the state." Petitioners made a house-to-house canvass of the 3,500 residents who lived north of the NPRR tracks and had filled twenty-two copies of the petition with signatures by the end of April 1937. The Missoula Chamber of Commerce also threw its support behind the effort, as did railroad officials in the Garden City.

The following month, a large delegation of Missoula residents traveled to Helena to present the petitions to the State Highway Commission and plead their case for the underpass. The Missoula group was one of sixteen delegations, including approximately two hundred individuals, that spoke to the highway commissioners at the meeting. "In every case, the representations of each delegation were attentively listened to and the requests submitted were taken under advisement." Apparently, the commissioners listened to the Missoula delegation more closely than the others. Two days after the meeting, they authorized highway department engineers to study the three proposed sites for the underpass.

The promise of 100 percent federal funding for the structure kept the momentum on the project going. On September 11, 1937, the State Highway Commission, a Bureau of Public Roads district engineer, NPRR officials and local representatives met in Missoula to discuss possible locations for the estimated $300,000 underpass. The group narrowed the possibilities down to two sites, with rights-of-way factors in the decision. The NPRR, the city and the highway commission favored Harris Street as the site of the new overpass. The highway commissioners told a *Missoulian* reporter that "the underpass will be of the most modern type of construction in the Northwest, and there will be nothing to match it in size or construction in the state."

By the end of September, the design of the structure was well underway in the Montana Highway Department's bridge section. On November 18, the Bureau of Public Roads approved the project statement for the underpass and the highway commissioners authorized acquisition of right-of-way for the structure. The preferred site would tunnel under twelve sets of railroad tracks, North First Street West and Railroad Street, the Pacific Fruit and Produce Company warehouse and a Northern Pacific freight warehouse. The project length on Harris Street (now Orange Street) would stretch 1,035 feet from West Alder Street to the south and North Second Street West on the north. The project required the acquisition of six dwellings. Highway department right-of-way agents were unable to come to terms with the owners of four properties, and all four properties were condemned by the court.

Advertisements for the "construction of a steel and concrete highway underpass of the Northern Pacific Railway Co. tracks at Harris Street… together with the construction of 0.210 miles of approach road and other subsidiary work" appeared in statewide newspapers and regional trade journals on March 16, 1938. Within a few days, contractors descended on Harris Street to investigate the project site prior to their submittal of proposals. The state highway commissioners opened ten bids for the project in their offices in Helena on March 31. The commissioners awarded the project to Miles City, Montana contractor Jerome C. Boespflug for his low bid of $226,531. His construction foreman, C.W. Miller, began staging for the project in mid-April. Paul Johnson, who had experience building underpasses in western Montana, served as the highway commission's resident engineer on the project.

Boespflug began excavation for the underpass on May 7, 1938. He employed two shifts on the project consisting of ten to twenty men each. By the end of the summer, sixty-five men were working on the project, all local residents hired from the local National Re-Employment Service office. The contractor brought in a second shovel to help remove over 26,000 cubic yards of dirt, which he hauled to the north end of the nearby Orange Street Bridge for storage. The Works Progress Administration used the fill dirt for projects in the Missoula area funded under that federal program. Through May, the workers dug under the NPRR freight warehouse and placed timbers to support the structure. Northern Pacific crews rerouted the tracks adjacent to

The Orange Street tunnel project was a major benefit for Missoula, meriting daily reports of its progress in the *Missoulian*. *Montana Rail Link Collection, Northern Pacific Railway Historical Association.*

its freight warehouse onto five temporary seven-span timber bridges to keep rail traffic moving. Boespflug employed "pumpcrete" on the project. From the mixing plant north of the construction site, concrete was "shot through a pipeline" 150 feet to the construction site. Aggregate for the concrete came from gravel pits along the Bitterroot River near Missoula. The Three Forks Cement Company at Trident in the Gallatin valley supplied twenty-eight railroad cars full of cement for the project.

Work on the underpass was complicated by the presence of twelve sets of railroad tracks, the freight depot and the Pacific Fruit and Produce Company warehouse located on the roof of the structure. Boespflug had to coordinate the excavation and pouring of concrete with the NPRR. Fortunately, the contractor and railroad worked well together when coordinating their efforts. At most, only three railroad tracks out of twelve could be utilized at a time. By mid-June, Boespflug had placed posts and beams under the fruit company's warehouse on the north half of the structure. The crews averaged pouring sixty cubic yards per day for the abutments of the underpass.

Construction of the underpass progressed through the summer of 1938 and was well-covered in the *Missoulian*. The steel for the structure's roof began arriving in Missoula the second week of July. Two carloads of structural steel arrived that week from Chicago. The contractor made arrangements with the NPRR for the use of a wrecker car to move the steel to the job site. Boespflug's crews placed "ten heavy steel girders, painted bright red, on the south abutment of the underpass." Boespflug installed heavy steel plates on top of the girders to support the railroad tracks. Excavation then began under the Pacific Fruit Company's warehouse on the north half of the underpass. By the end of July, the contractor had backfilled behind the east and west abutments of the underpass. On-the-job accidents, if any, were not reported in the *Missoulian*. Tragically, the foreman of the project's morning shift, Warren Smith, died of a heart attack at the job site on the morning of August 5.

By early September 1938, the underpass was little more than half complete, and work on it rapidly progressed. Boespflug's crews had begun working on the extensive number of concrete stairways from the top of the underpass to the street below. The workers completed the installation of ten-ton girders on the north side of the structure on October 24. The NPRR removed the temporary bridges, and normal rail operations resumed in late November. Boespflug had completed most of the underpass before bad weather forced a shutdown in work. By December 1, the underpass was 90 percent complete, with only concrete paving yet to be accomplished. An unanticipated problem at the project site arose in early January, when the job site's night watchman reported that flares placed at both ends of the underpass "disappear as fast as he [could] obtain replacements." The final phase of construction for the Orange Street Tunnel began in April 1939, when six-inch-thick concrete paving slabs were placed on the approaches to the underpass. Boespflug completed the underpass a couple days before the July 1, 1939 deadline for the project. When completed, the underpass was illuminated by eighty-six lights of different types and sizes.

The City of Missoula dedicated the new underpass on the morning of July 1, after the city's fiftieth golden jubilee parade. Elizabeth Crawshaw, a longtime advocate for the underpass, officially christened the underpass by breaking a bottle of Rattlesnake Creek water on the pavement in front of the south portal to the underpass and then cutting the ribbon, officially opening it to the people of Missoula. As the long concrete structure was formally opened to traffic, a stagecoach, accompanied by a band of whooping horseback riders from the jubilee parade, clattered through the underpass at full speed, adding a touch of the old Wild West to the christening of the modern pedestrian and automobile subway.

From Railroad Street above the south portal of the structure, Bureau of Public Roads district engineer Luce F. Martin officially presented the underpass to the City of Missoula. He introduced the men who were involved

The tunnel displays design features that distinguish it from similar structures in Montana. This includes decorative portals, arcaded sidewalks and warehouses on its roof. *HAER Photograph-MDT*.

in the building of the structure, including Boespflug, resident engineer Paul Johnson and members of the state highway commission. Mayor Dwight Mason stated that the underpass provided pedestrian access from all streets through stairways and ramps, eliminated two at-grade railroad crossings and was "the best lighted spot in Missoula for night traffic" because of its spotlights at each portal. The structure's completion marked the end of a thirty-year effort to provide a safe connection between the north and south sides of the Garden City.

Two days after the underpass was opened to traffic, the city received complaints about it. The *Missoulian* wrote that a "flaw [had] developed in the new underpass. [It] makes too much noise—at least when most of the hundreds of motorists who use it persist in honking their horns when in the tunnel, presumably because of the unusual and loud echoing sound which results." Because of the underpass's proximity to the Northern Pacific Hospital and area residents, the structure quickly became a nuisance. Police officers soon ticketed "those who use their horns excessively," a tradition that persists to the present day. The underpass also quickly became a hangout for teenage boys who sought to pick up the girls who walked on the sidewalks through the underpass. In 1949, the city installed blinking yellow lights to remind motorists of the fifteen-miles-per-hour speed limit through the underpass. At some point in the underpass's history, the city put in chain link fencing to prevent pedestrians from jumping into traffic from the arcade. The portal beams have occasionally been struck by over-height vehicles whose drivers ignored the clearance signs. In 2010, the City of Missoula hired a local artist to paint murals on the faces of the portals as part of a city beautification program.

ANCIENT LANDSCAPES

THE PRYOR MOUNTAINS
AND RAPTOR COUNTRY

The Pryor Mountains are located in south-central Montana in Carbon County and on the Crow Reservation. The prominent cliffs and dip slopes are composed of Madison limestone, which was deposited in shallow seas over three hundred million years ago. Along the margins of the mountains, younger tan-colored Tensleep sandstone and the brick-red Chugwater Formation crop out. Canyons in the range expose older rocks, including Precambrian basement rock that is more than two billion years old. Crustal blocks that form the Pryor Mountains were uplifted along reverse faults about fifty-five to sixty-five million years ago.

Over millions of years, water dissolved deep caves in the limestone. Some open vertically to the surface, allowing cold, dense air to sink down into the cave. The rock acts as an insulator, trapping the dense air and moisture underground, resulting in spectacular ice caves, such as Big Ice Cave. Other caves in the mountains have fantastic formations of stalagmites and stalactites.

About 115 million years ago, ten-foot-long dinosaurs with razor-sharp claws and teeth and retractable, slashing talons on their hind feet hunted in packs in this area. Lightly built, agile and quick, these intelligent carnivores could run at speeds of up to twenty-five miles per hour and were the perfect killing machines of their time. In 1964, on a windswept hill in the Badlands near the Pryor Mountains, Yale professor John Ostrom discovered the fossil remains of just such a creature. The discovery of this animal, called *Deinonychus antirrhopus* (or "terrible claw"), revolutionized the study of paleontology and

Top: Montana is a treasure trove of fossils. First found near the Pryor Mountains, a predator called *Deinonychus* revolutionized our understanding of dinosaurs. This skeletal mount is on display at the Field Museum of Natural History. *Photograph by Jonathan Chen, https://creativecommons.org/licenses/by-sa/4.0/.*

Bottom: An artist's restoration of *Deinonychus antirrhopus*. *Photgrapho by Fred Wierum, https://creativecommons.org/licenses/by-sa/4.0/.*

changed our understanding of dinosaurs. Because of its unique skeletal structure, the deinonychus had more in common with birds than it did reptiles. The great amount of energy it needed to survive has also led some to believe that it was warm-blooded rather than cold-blooded, like its reptilian cousins. Because of deinonychus, paleontologists now consider dinosaurs to have been agile, smart and social animals rather than slow-moving and dull-witted.

Fortunately for us, deinonychus died out millions of years ago and no longer scours these hills for prey.

The range is culturally important to the Apsaalooka (Crow) people and, according to tribal stories and beliefs, is the home of the Awakkulé, or "little people." Standing at only three feet tall, they are tremendously strong, said to be able to pack a whole elk on their shoulders. Aside from their abilities as hunters, they are also known to convey spiritual wisdom and blessings on individuals they deem worthy. The Awakkulé have had a significant influence on the history of the Apsaalooka, providing them with spiritual knowledge and protection.

20

A DREAM COME TRUE

The Fred Robinson Bridge

On August 16, 1959, over five thousand people converged in automobiles, airplanes and boats at a remote site on the Missouri River, about sixty miles northeast of Lewistown. They were there to celebrate the opening of a new bridge across the river, the culmination of a forty-year effort by residents of the area to build it. The structure was later designated the Fred Robinson Bridge by grateful Montanans for the man who worked hardest to get it built.

Beginning in 1920, businessmen, ranchers and farmers from Fergus, Blaine and Phillips Counties joined together to push for the construction of a bridge across the Missouri River between Malta and Lewistown. Six ferries in that 430-mile stretch of river provided the only crossing between Fort Benton and Fort Peck, and they operated seasonally. The campaign gained momentum in 1922, when members of the group pushing for a bridge elected influential Lewistown newspaperman Tom Stout as chairman of a committee that was to pressure the Montana Highway Commission into building it. By 1929, the committee had gained sufficient influence in the Montana legislature to direct the highway commission "to make necessary examinations and surveys preliminary to the location for construction of [a] highway bridge over the Missouri [River]."

The commission presented its report to the legislature in 1931. Of the six Missouri River sites they investigated, the commissioners recommended two to the legislature: the Power Plant site southwest of Hays and the Rocky Point site near Wilder Crossing south of Malta. Because of the lower overall cost of the project and the more direct connection between the Hi-Line, Lewistown and Billings, the commissioners chose the Rocky Point site as their preferred location. Before the legislature could take action, however, Montana was plunged into the Great Depression, which temporarily ended any serious consideration of the bridge for the foreseeable future. Despite that, delegations from Phillips, Blaine and Fergus Counties met occasionally with the commission about the bridge. One of the representatives involved was state senator Fred Robinson of Phillips County.

Born in Tennessee in 1889, Fred Robinson came to Montana in 1911 and took up a homestead claim north of Wagner in Phillips County. He worked on the Milk River Irrigation Project and owned a general store in Wagner before he enlisted in the army during World War I. Upon his discharge and return to Montana, he served as the Phillips County assessor and co-owned an automobile dealership in Malta. In 1936, voters elected him to the Montana State Senate, a position he held until his retirement in 1960.

In January 1945, Robinson, with help of the media and legislators from his region, successfully lobbied the Twenty-Ninth Legislature to pass House Joint Resolution 1, essentially a reiteration of its 1929 ruling regarding the bridge. The highway department bridge engineers developed a modern seven-span steel girder design for the structure and conducted an economic study of the bridge's benefits. Despite all the work put into the project, the commission did not have enough money to build the structure. Consequently, the Lewistown-based Missouri River Bridge Association and the Highway 19 Association from Malta aggressively sought new financial options, including the possibility of building a toll bridge. Senator Robinson claimed that the bonds raised to build the bridge could be retired after fifteen years if the state charged two dollars per passenger vehicle. He added that the people in central and north-central Montana wanted the bridge so badly that it did not matter where it was built, just as long as it was built. The passion of the bridge's promoters impressed Montana governor John Bonner. He ordered the highway commission to conduct yet another study to find a way to finance the bridge as soon as possible. The toll bridge idea never materialized, as the commissioners found a way to finance the bridge. Because the site of the proposed bridge was partially located within the Charles M. Russell National Wildlife Refuge, the federal government would pay the full cost of the structure.

In October 1956, the highway commission awarded a contract to the Sheridan, Wyoming–based N.A. Nelson Construction Company. The project, however, proved a logistical nightmare for the contractor. The construction site was located thirty-one miles from the nearest railroad terminal at Roy. The building material had to be trucked in from Roy on a "trail of the worst kind of gumbo imaginable." The materials could be hauled only during periods of dry weather. Nelson established a trailer camp near the bridge site, which is currently the Bureau of Land Management's James Kipp Campground. To accommodate the workers, the company drilled a well, laid water and sewer pipes and built a small electric light plant. Despite the amenities, the contractor's superintendent, Earl Rook, later remembered that he "had more trouble keeping experienced men on the job than on any job he [had] ever built."

The contractor installed two concrete mixers, a three-bin aggregate batcher and steam boilers near the bridge's south abutment. The firm also built a temporary timber trestle on the upstream side of the site that provided access to the pier foundations. Once the foundations had been excavated, the contractor used an electric tram to transport the concrete from the mixers to the point of delivery. The contractor worked two eight-hour shifts per day

At 698 feet in length and bearing on three massive reinforced concrete piers, the Fred Robinson Bridge is an imposing landmark in central Montana. *MHS Photograph Archives, Helena, PAc 86-15 100B.*

Around five thousand people attended the dedication of the bridge, the culmination of a thirty-year effort, in 1959. *MHS Photograph Archives, Helena, PAc 86-15 121 A52.*

while excavating the foundations. Workers completed the bridge's concrete substructure in December 1957.

The structural steel did not arrive in Roy until June 1958. Because the roads were nearly impassable, the contractor could not begin trucking the steel to the construction site until the end of the month. To meet the contract deadline, the Nelson Company expanded its work schedule to nine-hour days six or seven days a week. The company opened the bridge for traffic on March 27, 1959. The final cost of the structure was $716,633.

As with most major bridge projects in Montana history, those impacted most by it planned an elaborate ceremony to dedicate the structure. The dedication ceremonies occurred four and a half months later on August 16.

Chief Justice James Harrison was master of ceremonies at the event, which included speeches by many Montanan and Canadian dignitaries, including Montana governor J. Hugo Aronson and Senator Fred Robinson. A local radio station broadcast the proceedings live throughout central Montana. Robinson provided six steers for a barbecue, with other food and condiments supplied by community organizations throughout the region. Bands from Malta, Chinook and Havre provided live entertainment for the celebrants.

Governor Aronson and Robinson symbolically opened the bridge by sawing a cottonwood log in half at the structure's north end. Speeches were given at a speaking platform that was set up at the south end of the bridge. After Stout's opening speech about the history of the campaign to build the bridge, he was followed by mostly self-congratulatory addresses by the other speakers. Montana Highway Department chief engineer Fred Quinnell praised Senator Robinson and his associates for their "courage, persistence, and perseverance to make the dream a reality." The Fred Robinson Bridge concluded a thirty-nine-year effort by central Montanans to provide a connection between the north and south sides of the Missouri River. The bridge's significance manifested itself in the thousands of people who attended the event at the remote site in north-central Montana.

The Fred Robinson Bridge celebrated its sixtieth birthday in 2019. Although it has been plagued by slides on the north side of the Missouri River and increasing traffic, the bridge is an important landmark in central Montana. Few today, however, remember the efforts it took Montanans to get the bridge built and its continuing significance to central Montana's economy. It not only opened up the region to agricultural development but also provided an important "take out" place for hundreds of people who float the Upper Missouri National Wild and Scenic River. It is truly a monument above the water.

MONTANA ROADSIDES

THE SPRINGDALE CUT

Few would argue that the interstate highway system has not had an enormous impact on the United States and Montana. President Dwight Eisenhower signed the legislation that created the program in June 1956. It was the culmination of a decades-long effort by the Bureau of Public Roads, the American Association of State Highway Officials, state highway departments and others to create a true transcontinental controlled-access highway system. Under the legislation, the federal government would pay 92 percent of the costs of the system. Certain design standards had to be met, including a minimum design speed of seventy miles per hour (fifty miles per hour in mountainous terrain), controlled access, interchanges and standardized overpasses. The interstate highway program remains the largest public works program in U.S. history.

Montana began planning for an interstate highway system as early as 1941, when the highway commission designated a defense highway network during World War II. The approximate routes of today's interstates in Montana had been set by 1947, when the commission designated the National System of Interstate Highways. With Eisenhower's signing of the Federal Highway Act of 1956, the Montana Highway Department began an ambitious expansion program that included the formation of an Interstate Highway Division and a five-story addition onto the old highway department's headquarters at the corner of North Roberts Street and East Sixth Avenue, across from the state capitol building, in Helena. The department doubled its size in personnel and budget from 1957 to 1959, when the first interstate highways were built.

At first glance, you'd think the interstate program would have been met with public approval. It did in some sectors, but it was decidedly unpopular in others—largely by the people who would be most impacted by it. The big problem was right-of-way acquisition. It was a problem not just in Montana but across the United States. Rights-of-way delayed projects. Landowners were often loath to sell their property for a four-lane, controlled-access highway in rural Montana. The problem was compounded by the highway engineers at the time who designed the roads by taking the path of least resistance. This meant that interstate alignments often went right down the middle of valleys, splitting farms and ranches in two. The problem became a major bone of contention in the Yellowstone valley between Livingston and Laurel. Between 1958 and 1965, the highway commission initiated several condemnation proceedings against landowners along the proposed route of Interstate 90.

Another issue was the huge amount of federal funding flowing into the state for the interstate system. Many lawmakers and citizens believed the highway department was wasting or misspending the federal largesse. This was a mistaken public impression that the highway commission and Chief Highway Engineer Fred Quinnell Jr. actively fought against. The interstates were big news in Montana in the late 1950s and early 1960s, with considerable news coverage in local newspapers and on editorial pages. It seemed the interstates polarized many Montanans into two groups: those who welcomed the freeways and those who didn't.

The first major interstate project that garnered a lot of attention from the media was the construction of I-90 east of Livingston. One segment became a poster child for all that many believed was wrong with the system. But it also represented the very best in highway engineering, as it placed a four-lane highway in a constricted environment. Interstate 90 is the longest interstate highway in the United

States, stretching three thousand miles from Seattle, Washington, to Buffalo, Massachusetts. In Montana, it is 552 miles long and replaced parts of U.S. 10 and U.S. 87 as the busiest highway in the state. The construction of I-15 was a priority for the highway commission, the first two segments let to contract being the bridges on Billings's south side and the four-mile segment in Park County between Big Timber and Livingston in April 1958.

The Big Timber–Livingston contract was controversial. The highway commission awarded a $1.5 million contract to the Albert LaLonde Construction Company of Sidney, Montana, to construct a little over four miles of a controlled-access two-lane interstate between Livingston and Big Timber. Construction on the project was started in May, but by December, it had become glaringly obvious there was a problem along the Yellowstone River, where a major cut was under construction. Prior to the letting of the contract, the highway department hired a consultant to do a geotechnical investigation at the proposed cut site. It reported back to the highway department engineers that the site was mostly composed of solid rock. Consequently, the engineers designed a backslope. When Lalonde began the construction of the cut, however, it discovered that it wasn't quite solid rock; there were layers of shale and other unstable materials mixed in. The contractor found that "upon being disturbed, the formation created a definite hazard to workmen, equipment, and the traveling public due to falling rocks and slides caused by rains and erosion." Lalonde immediately ceased work on the road cut.

The engineers quickly redesigned the backslopes, laying them back to a one-and-a-half-to-one slope to eliminate the danger. The highway commissioners issued a change order to the LaLonde Company for $198,000 and followed it up with a supplemental contract to the contractor for $1.1 million to fix the cut, now known in the press and political circles as the Springdale Cut in honor of the nearby community. The problem, ultimately, was that

The Springdale Cut under construction. The landscape feature is a remnant of the early days of the interstate highway construction program. *MHS Photograph Archives, Helena, PAc 86-15 18C.*

the highway commission, at the recommendation of Chief Engineer Quinnell, did not advertise a revised contract for the work. The timing couldn't have been worse; this took place just before a legislative session. The cut's fill material hit the proverbial fan.

In January 1959, representative Truman Bradford, a freshman Democrat from Cascade County, formed a House Special Investigating Committee to look into what he and his fellow committee members believed was waste, mismanagement and poor planning on the part of the highway department and highway commission. Ben Stein, a Democrat from Park County, was a member of the committee and a vocal opponent to the highway department and, especially, Quinnell. The committee received considerable publicity, much of it negative, from supporters of the interstate program and politicians in Montana newspapers.

During the course of the investigation, the highway department revealed that it did not have the proper equipment to core drill the hillside. Consequently, it had to contract with a private consultant to conduct the study. No excuses were made for the geotechnical consultant, and the highway department had to go with the results it received from the company. Ben Stein, however, was not satisfied with Quinnell's explanation and demanded the Federal Bureau of Public Roads conduct an investigation into the issue. The bureau refused, stating that there was nothing to investigate. Herb Lees, a member of the Livingston Chamber of Commerce's Highway Committee, claimed Stein was stirring up trouble for his own political advantage. Indeed, the Springdale Cut would be the basis of a feud between Stein and Quinnell that would later spill over into the next big interstate highway project in the Wolf Creek Canyon in 1961. Quinnell made no secret of his dislike of Representative Stein. He tacked a portrait of the legislator on his office wall and threw darts at it.

Meanwhile, the LaLonde Company continued work on the Springdale Cut. In August 1960, the contractor began surfacing the four-mile interstate segment and just needed to install the median barrier, stripe the road and install the signage. By October, LaLonde had completed the work. The project took two years to complete and involved the removal of 1.8 million cubic yards of dirt and rock. The *Livingston Enterprise* reported that the segment had become "one of the most popular drives around Livingston." The controversy surrounding the project didn't immediately die down, however. The U.S. General Accounting Office looked into the project and repeated almost verbatim the conclusions drawn by the Bradford Committee. Chief Engineer Quinnell responded that the highway department had "been constantly harassed by a small, highly audible minority that seems to want to hamstring the road-building program in Montana." He stated that the department had gone as far as to form

The Springdale Cut east of Livingston is striking evidence of Interstate 90's impact on Montana's landscape. *Rob Park/MDT.*

a special section to answer criticism about the interstate program largely because of this project. In 1964, Quinnell left the highway department. Ben Stein lost his seat in the state legislature in 1971.

The Springdale Cut stands as a significant interstate-related landscape feature next to I-90, about thirteen miles east of Livingston between mileposts 350 to 351. It symbolizes the change in road building that occurred because of the interstate highway program. In the past, the two-lane primaries largely conformed to the landscape. The interstates changed the landscape to make it accommodate them. It is an impressive landmark that still generates comments from motorists on Montana's busiest interstate highway.

21

STEEL TRACKS TO MONTANA'S PAST

Montana's Centennial Train, 1964

The Montana Department of Transportation (MDT) has been a major player in many different things since its creation in 1913—not all of them involved construction and maintenance of Montana's highway system. Some, like the official highway map, make sense; while others, like its acquisition of the Pictograph Cave site outside Billings in 1938, might seem like a stretch for a department dedicated to improving and maintaining the state's roads and bridges. But for nearly fifty years, the department was involved in advertising the state as a tourist destination. The roadside historical markers, museums, roadside picnic areas, port of entry stations and tourism literature and road maps are all examples of the MDT's efforts to draw visitors to the Big Sky Country by advertising the state's colorful and scenic recreational attractions and history. The MDT retained that responsibility until 1975, when the State Advertising Department became part of the Department of Commerce, where it resides today.

In 1963, Montana chambers of commerce, civic clubs, the Montana Historical Society and other organizations began planning for the celebration of the centennial of Montana Territory. Because the Montana Highway Department oversaw the State Advertising Department, it became involved in the preparations for the centennial. Along with the beard-growing and costume contests, parades and historical pageants, the centerpiece of the celebration was to be the Montana Centennial Train. The train was the brainchild of two men, Howard Kelsey and Jack Hume, who saw an opportunity to celebrate the centennial and promote the state to would-be visitors from all over the country. The men garnered the financial support of individuals, businessmen and state agencies, including the highway department.

Backers of the project purchased nine railcars in West Virginia, with the Northern Pacific and Burlington Railroads loaning an additional sixteen cars and a locomotive. The interiors of the railcars were filled with exhibit cases rich in historical artifacts and artwork loaned by the Montana Historical Society. Kelsey and Hume planned a monthlong goodwill tour that would begin on April 5, 1964, and stop in nine cities before arriving at the New York World's Fair in time for Montana Day on April 22. The train would remain on display there for three days before returning to Montana on May 5. Three hundred passengers, characterized as "gregarious, happy, fun-loving Montanans," paid for the privilege of riding on the train and included cowboys, Natives, musicians, Miss Montana Centennial and Montana governor Tim Babcock and his wife, Betty. Seventy-two horses would also accompany the group, along with a chuck wagon, Conestoga wagon "and other vehicles of ancient vintage." In other words (and according to firsthand accounts), it was a party train. The only thing remaining was to decorate the exterior of the train.

In June 1963, Kelsey and Hume appeared before the Montana State Highway Commission, explained their plans and asked the commissioners for help. It was quick in coming. The commissioners appropriated $30,000 in state funds for the production of fifty-four paintings that would decorate the exterior of the train on its cross-country tour of the United States. Artists Lyman Rice and Bud Wert painted the eight-by-sixteen-foot murals on behalf of the highway commission, which then loaned them to the Centennial

The exterior of the Centennial Train was lavishly decorated with paintings depicting Montana scenery and wildlife. *MDT.*

The interior of the Centennial Train featured artifacts associated with Montana's history and western paintings by famed cowboy artist Charlie Russell. *MHS Photograph Archives, Helena, PAc 86-15 C-57-B.*

Train until the tour was completed. Thereafter, the commissioners planned to display the panels, which depicted Montana from prehistory through the nineteenth century, at highway rest areas.

What the commissioners didn't anticipate was that they'd become financially responsible for the train. In October 1963, Governor Babcock asked that the finances of the train be taken over by the highway commission, which would give it the legal authority to operate beyond the June 30, 1965 expiration of the Territorial Centennial Commission. One commissioner, George Gosman of Dillon, wasn't happy with the arrangement, and he claimed, "We're going to be parents of the train, but let the [centennial commission] run it as they damn please. It doesn't look like a business transaction at all." The commissioners directed State Advertising director Orvin Fjare, an employee of the highway department, that he would be responsible for the operation of the train, and the department's accountant, Robert O'Leary, would manage the centennial commission's finances. Somewhere along the line, the highway department obtained ownership of nine railcars. The Centennial Train became the unwanted adopted baby of the highway commission.

After touring several Montana cities in late March and early April 1964, the train left Billings for New York on April 5, stopping at Omaha; Kansas City; St. Louis; Louisville; Cincinnati; Charleston; Washington, D.C.; Baltimore; and Philadelphia before arriving at the World's Fair on April 22. By all accounts, the passengers had a ball. Future governor Judy Martz, a 1964 winter Olympics speed skater, worked as a hostess on the train. The tour was a resounding success and returned to Billings on May 5 after stopping in six cities in the Midwest. Once the excitement of the trip cooled, however, the question for the highway commissioners became: What do we do with the Centennial Train?

The highway department removed the murals from the exterior of the train and put them in storage at its Billings district office. The nine core railroad cars were mothballed at the Laurel railyard, where they stayed for the next seven years. Finally, in 1971, the highway commissioners leased some of the railcars to communities for use as tourist information centers. The cars ended up in Hungry Horse, Wibaux, West Yellowstone, Glasgow and Gardiner. Eventually, many of the murals were sold to private collectors or donated to local museums throughout Montana; four were kept for display in the new highway department building in the 1980s. Today, two Centennial Train cars can still be seen in Wibaux and West Yellowstone. It is not known what happened to many of the murals.

BIBLIOGRAPHY

Axline, Jon. *Taming Big Sky Country: The History of Montana Transportation from Trails to Interstates*. Charleston, SC: The History Press, 2015.

Hanchett, Lee, Jr. *Montana's Benton Road*. Wolf Creek, MT: Pine Rim Publishing, 2008.

Meeks, Harold A. *On the Road to Yellowstone: The Yellowstone Trail and American Highways, 1900–1930*. Missoula, MT: Pictorial Histories Publishing Co. Inc., 2000.

Montana Place Names from Alzada to Zortman: A Montana Historical Society Guide. Helena: Montana Historical Society Press, 2009.

Moulton, Gary E., ed. *The Definitive Journals of Lewis & Clark: From Fort Mandan to Three Forks*. Vol. 4. Lincoln: University of Nebraska Press, 2002.

Paladin, Vivian A. *Valleys of the Prickly Pear*. Helena, MT: Little Red Schoolhouse, 1988.

Reeder, George C., ed. *Theodore Roosevelt International Highway*. Glasgow, MT: Glasgow Courier, 1921.

Ridge, John, and Alice Ridge. *Introducing the Yellowstone Trail: A Good Road from Plymouth Rock to Puget Sound, 1912–1930*. Altoona, WI: Yellowstone Trail Association, 2000.

Schussler, Edith. *Doctors, Dynamite and Dogs*. Caldwell, ID: Caxton Printers, 1956.

Shontz, John. *Taft: The Story of the St. Paul Pass Tunnel and America's Wickedest City*. Antioch, IL: Milwaukee Road Heritage Association, 2022.

Twain, Mark. *Roughing It*. New York: Pocket Books, 2003.

Urbaniak, Timothy. *Men of the Cave: The Excavation of Empty Gulch*. Billings: Self-published, 2022.

Newspapers

Anaconda Standard
Billings Daily Tribune
Billings Gazette
Butte Daily Post
Butte Miner
Carbon County News
Circle Banner
Dillon Examiner
Great Falls Tribune
Helena Independent
Helena Record Herald
Kalispell Daily Inter Lake
Missoulian
Montana Standard

National Register of Historic Places Nominations

Beavertown Stage Station
Black Otter Trail
Browne's Bridge
Dearborn River High Bridge
Fred Robinson Bridge
Gladstone Hotel
Harding Way
Hepburn's Museum
Lewis and Clark County Poor Farm
MacDonald Pass Airway Beacon
Matt's Place
Morelli Bridge
Orange Street Tunnel
Tower Rock

INDEX

ABOUT THE AUTHOR

Jon Axline is the longtime historian at the Montana Department of Transportation. Among his many responsibilities at the department, he writes roadside historical and geological interpretive markers. Jon has contributed to *Montana Magazine* and *Montana: The Magazine of Western History*. He is the author of *Conveniences Sorely Needed: Montana's Historic Highway Bridges* and the editor of *Montana's Historical Highway Markers*, *Taming Big Sky Country: A History of Montana Transportation from Trails to Interstates* and *The Beartooth Highway: A History of America's Most Beautiful Drive*, *Montana Highway Tales: Curious Characters, Historic Sites and Peculiar Attractions*. He coauthored *Hidden Helena* with his good friend and colleague Ellen Baumler. Jon lives in Helena with his wife and five dogs.

Visit us at
www.historypress.com